# ELEMENTS OF
MEDICAL LAW

Printed by: Antony Rowe Ltd, Chippenham, Wiltshire

# ELEMENTS OF MEDICAL LAW

**Charles Foster**

**Of the Inner Temple, Barrister**

Barry Rose Law Publishers Limited
Little London
Chichester

© 2005 Charles Foster and Barry Rose Law Publishers Limited

ISBN 1 902681 53 3

All rights reserved. No part of this publication may be reproduced, stored in a retrieval system, or transmitted in any form or by any means, electronic, mechanical, photocopying, recording or otherwise, without prior written permission of the author, publishers and Copyright Licensing Agency Ltd.

**Barry Rose Law Publishers Limited**
**Little London, Chichester**

# CONTENTS

| | |
|---|---|
| Preface | vii |
| Acknowledgments | ix |
| Statutes | x |
| Statutory Instruments | xi |
| Cases Cited | xii |
| | |
| Chapter 1: Legal Issues Before Birth | 1 |
| Chapter 2: Consent | 35 |
| Chapter 3: Confidentiality | 67 |
| Chapter 4: Clinical Negligence | 88 |
| Chapter 5: The Law of Death | 142 |
| Appendix 1: Particulars of Claim in a Clinical Negligence Case | 178 |
| Appendix 2: Defence in a Clinical Negligence Case | 183 |
| Index | 189 |

# PREFACE

This book stems from a number of convictions.

First: medical law is nothing like as difficult as practitioners in the field (like myself) pretend that it is. There are lots of intimidating and very good books on medical law which bristle with footnotes. Unless you are one of the cognoscenti, those books are unreadably thorough: you would never be able to sketch your own mental map of the subject from wandering through them. There are just a few landmarks in the subject. Fix them, and you will be able to take your own line across country on most medical law matters.

Second: medical law is far and away the most fascinating corner of the law. It deals with life and before it, and death and after it. There's not much left. The cases which illuminate it are the most tragic and happy and colourful, as the medico-legally obsessed tabloids agree.

Third: medical law matters. It is bound to, given its scope. It says a lot about what society thinks is the essence of a human being. Other areas of law hint at this: medical law is forced to say it directly.

Fourth: medical law is utterly incoherent. It is a sort of philosophical pick and mix. If you are kind you put that down to pragmatism. If you are not you sometimes put it down to intellectual dishonesty and sometimes to downright sloppiness. The law is old, and too often gives old answers to new problems. Medicine is evolving fast, throwing down new philosophical gauntlets to the law as it does. The law is sometimes too tired to pick them up.

Fifth: it is possible for the law to be more coherent than it is. There are some principles which appear everywhere. They are mostly ethical: like a respect for human autonomy, and a realisation that autonomy has limits.

I have tried to give the co-ordinates of the main landmarks. The book should therefore be useful to anyone who wants to know something about the black-letter law; whether student, practising lawyer, doctor or interested layman. I have also dealt in more detail than a student's crammer would want with the difficult and controversial cases, asking what if any principles drove the judges concerned, and commenting on ethical and legal discordances with other cases. You can't just brush the case of the conjoined twins under the forensic carpet, commenting that hard cases make bad law, as if that were a reputable philosophical position. It will certainly come crawling back out at an embarrassing time if you do. Nor is it good enough to keep the case in a museum of legal monstrosities, to be peered at for entertainment outside working hours. Better to see where it comes from and where it is going. If you decide that the doctors who withdrew Tony Bland's feeding tube aren't murderers because the withdrawal was an omission, you can't object loudly, or at any rate honestly, if obviously murderous omissions go unpunished. Better to look at whether there is a real distinction between acts and omissions, and if so or if not, what to do about it.

I have failed, of course, but at least I had a go.

The law is as I reckon it is in February 2005.


**Charles Foster,**
**Temple,**
**London EC4**

# ACKNOWLEDGMENTS

Every law book is woven from the ideas of thousands of people. The legislators and the judges do the main strands, and then everyone the writer talks to contributes something to the rest. All barristers spend a lot of their lives wandering into their colleagues' rooms and asking them for their view on things. So I owe a lot to the patient barristers at 6 Pump Court, as well as to my opponents at the medical bar. Professor Tony Hope and Professor Mike Parker at Oxford have helped me to look at some of these problems through the eyes of clinical ethicists, and convinced me that promiscuous cross-fertilisation between ethical theory and law is necessary to produce a medico-legal creature with enough hybrid vigour to deal with the exhausting and exciting challenges of medical advance.

Some parts of some sections appeared in some form in articles by me in the *Solicitors Journal*, the *New Law Journal* and *Counsel* magazine. I am very grateful to the publishers for permission to reproduce parts of those articles. No one could ask for a more congenial publisher than Barry Rose or for a more friendly and efficient editing team than Gabi Fleet's. I am really very grateful to them all.

Much of this book was written in David Monteath's house in southern Poland, in between episodes of misanthropic pacing. His hospitality and long-suffering were crucial.

But Mary, a doctor who will never need any help from anyone in my corner of the law, bore the brunt of my moodiness and absence. This book is dedicated to her.

# STATUTES

| | |
|---|---|
| Abortion Act 1967 | 10, 15-17, 27 |
| Access to Health Records Act 1990 | 82 |
| Access to Medical Reports Act 1988 | 82 |
| Congenital Disabilities (Civil Liability) Act 1976 | 19-21, 23-4 |
| Consumer Protection Act 1987 | 135 |
| Corneal Tissue Act 1986 | 173 |
| Criminal Damage Act 1971 | 155 |
| Criminal Procedure (Attendance of Witnesses) Act 1965 | 79 |
| Criminal Procedure and Investigations Act 1996 | 79 |
| Data Protection Act 1998 | 81-3 |
| Family Law Reform Act 1969 | 53, 175 |
| Freedom of Information Act 2000 | 84-6 |
| Health and Social Care Act 2001 | 3, 84 |
| Human Fertilisation and Embryology Act 1990 | 6-12 |
| Human Organ Transplants Act 1989 | 174, 175-7 |
| Human Reproductive Cloning Act 2001 | 13 |
| Human Rights Act 1998 | 60-6, 86, 115-17, 151 |
| Human Tissue Act 1961 | 173-4 |
| Limitation Act 1980 | 136-7 |
| Mental Health Act 1983 | 54, 138 |
| National Health Service Act 1977 | 78, 97-9, 178 |
| National Health Service and Community Care Act 1990 | 178 |
| Offences Against the Person Act 1861 | 14, 37, 38 |
| Police and Criminal Evidence Act 1984 | 78 |
| Prevention of Terrorism (Temporary Provisions) Act 1989 | 78 |
| Public Health (Control of Disease) Act 1984 | 77 |
| Road Traffic Act 1988 | 4, 78 |
| Supreme Court Act 1981 | 181 |
| Theft Act | 7 |

# STATUTORY INSTRUMENTS

| | |
|---|---|
| Abortion Regulations 1991 (SI 1991/499) | 77 |
| Civil Procedure Rules | 183 |
| Data Protection (Subject Access Modification) (Health) Order 2000 (SI 2000/413) | 82 |
| Human Fertilisation and Embryology (Research) Regulations 2001 (SI 2001/188) | 13 |
| National Health Service (Notification of Births and Deaths) Regulations 1982 (SI 1982/286) | 78 |
| National Health Service (Venereal Diseases) Regulations 1974 | 4 |
| Patents (Amendment) Rules 2001 (SI 2001/1412) | 5 |
| Patents and Plant Variety Rights (Compulsory Licensing) Regulations 2002 (SI 2002/247) | 5 |
| Patents Regulations 2000 (SI 2000/2037) | 5, 6 |
| Public Health (Infectious Diseases) Regulations 1998 (SI 1998/1546) | 77 |

*International Legislation*

| | |
|---|---|
| European Convention on Human Rights | 20, 27-34, 35, 60-6, 86-7, 109, 115-17, 142, 153-4, 161-2, 166-9 |
| Art.2 | 14, 27-34, 66, 115-17, 166-7 |
| Art.3 | 27-8, 62-5, 161, 166-7, 169, 171 |
| Art.6 | 153 |
| Art.7 | 153 |
| Art.8 | 4, 8, 27-8, 60-2, 64-6, 72, 81-2, 85-7, 166-8, 171 |
| Art.8(1) | 60, 61, 71-2, 86, 168 |
| Art 8(2) | 60-1, 71-2, 86, 168 |
| European Council Directive 85/3275/EEC (consumer protection) | 135-6 |
| European Council Directive 98/44/EC | 5 |
| Orviedo Convention on Human Rights and Biomedicine | 31, 34 |
| United Nations Convention on the Rights of the Child | 62 |

# CASES CITED

A, Re (Conjoined Twins: Medical Treatment)
[2001] Fam 147     20, 145-52
A, Re (Medical Treatment: Male Sterilisation)
[2000] 1 FCR 193     56
A, Re (Minor)[1992] 3 Med LR 303     142
A v. National Blood Authority (No.1) [2001] 3 All ER 289     135
Acmanne     61
Airedale NHS Trust v. Bland [1993] 4 Med LR 39;
[1993] AC 789     18, 36, 59, 107, 111, 156-65, 172
Alcock v. Chief Constable of South Yorkshire [1992] 1 AC 310     95
Andersson (Anne-Marie) v. Sweden 25 EHRR 722     87
Appleton v. Garrett [1997] 8 Med LR 75     42
Associated Provincial Picture Houses Ltd v. Wednesbury
Corporation [1948] 1 KB 223     98
Attorney-General's Reference (No.3 of 1994) [1996] QB 581     15

B, In Re (Minor) (Wardship: Medical Treatment)
[1981] 1 WLR 1421     110
B v. An NHS Trust [2002] 2 All ER 449     40-1, 50
Barkway v. South Wales Transport [1950] 1 All ER 392     119
Board of Governors for the Hospitals for Sick Children v.
McLaughlin & Harvey Plc 19 Con LR 25     106
Bolam v. Friern Hospital Management Committee
[1957] 1 WLR 582     43-4, 46, 55-6, 65-6, 76, 100-8, 109, 112, 115-17, 121-2, 141, 152, 159-60, 166-7
Bolitho v. City and Hackney Health Authority
[1998] AC 232     43-4, 101-4, 109, 113, 121-2
Bonnington Castings v. Wardlaw [1956] AC 613     132
Boso v. Italy (2002) No.50490/99     27
Bull v. Devon Area Health Authority [1993] 4 Med LR 117     119-20

C, Re (Adult: Refusal of Treatment) [1994] 1 WLR 290     49-50
C, Re (Minor) (Medical Treatment) [1998] Lloyd's Rep Med 1     106
C, Re (Minor) (Wardship: Medical Treatment) [1990] Fam 26     110

Calver v. Westwood Veterinary Group [2001]
Lloyd's Rep Med 20 103
Caparo Industries plc v. Dickman [1990] 2 AC 605 93
Chaplin v. Hicks [1911] 2 KB 786 123, 126
Chatterton v. Gerson [1981] QB 432 41-2, 59
Chester v. Afshar [2004] UKHL 41 29, 133-4
Copp v. Chief Constable of Avon and Somerset Police
(1997) CLY 97/463 80

D v. UK (1997) 24 EHRR 423 169
Davies v. Taylor [1974] AC 207 126
Davis v. Barking, Havering and Brentwood Health Authority
[1993] 4 Med LR 85 42
Delaney v. Southmead Health Authority [1995] 6 Med LR 355 119
Dudley v. Stephens (1884) 14 QBD 273 148, 151

Early v. Newham Health Authority [1994] 5 Med LR 214 107
East African Asians Cases (1973) 3 EHRR 76 62
Ellis v. Home Office [1953] 2 QB 135 81
Emeh v. Kensington and Chelsea and Westminster Area
Health Authority [1985] QB 1012 25

F v. West Berkshire Health Authority
[1989] 2 All ER 545 55-6, 57, 61
Fairchild v. Glenhaven Funeral Services [2002] 3 WLR 89;
[2003] 1 AC 32 128-9, 132-4
Fothergill v. Monarch Airlines Ltd [1981] AC 251 153

Garcia v. Switzerland App No.10148/82 ECtHR 62
GF, *Re* [1992] 1 FLR 293 59
Gillick v. West Norfolk and Wisbech Area Health Authority
[1986] AC 112; [1985] 3 All ER 402 51, 52-3, 54, 150
Goodwill v. British Pregnancy Advisory Service
[1996] 2 All ER 161 94
Grayned v. City of Rockford 408 US 104 153
Gregg v. Scott [2005] UKHL 2 124-5, 130-1, 134
Guerra and others v. Italy (1998) 26 EHRR 357 65

| | |
|---|---|
| H v. Norway (1992) 73 DR 155 | 27 |
| Hashmi case | 9, 10-13 |
| Herczegfalvy v. Austria (1993) 15 EHRR 437 | 62-3 |
| Hotson v. East Berkshire Health Authority [1987] AC 750 | 122-4, 129 |
| Ireland v. UK (1978) 2 EHRR 25 | 62 |
| J, Re (Minor) (Wardship: Medical Treatment) [1991] Fam 33 | 110, 172 |
| Judge v. Huntingdon Health Authority (1996) 6 Med LR 223 | 124 |
| Kapfund v. Abbey National plc and Daniel [1999] 2 Lloyd's Rep Med 48 | 94 |
| Keenan v. UK (2001) 33 EHRR 913 | 169 |
| Kitchen v. Royal Air Force Association [1958] 1 WLR 563 | 126 |
| L, Re (Patient: Non-consensual Treatment) [1997] 8 Med LR 217 | 51 |
| Loveday v. Renton [1990] 1 Med LR 117 | 105 |
| Malette v. Shulman (1990) 67 DLR (4th) 321 | 40, 57 |
| Mallett v. McMonagle [1970] AC 166 | 126 |
| Maynard v. West Midlands Regional Health Authority [1984] 1 WLR 634 | 102 |
| MB, Re (Adult: Medical Treatment) [1997] 2 FCR 541; [1997] 8 Med LR 217 | 50, 56 |
| McFarlane v. Tayside Health Board [2000] AC 59 | 25-6 |
| McGhee v. NCB [1973] 1 WLR 1 | 132 |
| McKay v. Essex Area Health Authority [1982] QB 1166 | 21, 23, 24 |
| Mercer v. St Helens and Knowsley Hospitals NHS Trust (1995) CLY 95/4124 | 80 |
| Mobilio [1991] 1 VR 339 | 38 |
| MS v. Sweden 23 EHRR 313 | 87 |
| National Health Service Trust v. D [2000] 2 FLR 677 | 110 |
| National Health Service Trust A v. M [2001] 2 WLR 942 | 65, 166 |
| North West Lancashire Health Authority v. A, D and G [2000] 1 WLR 977 | 110 |

| | |
|---|---|
| Osman v. UK [1999] 1 FLR 193 | 116 |
| Page v Smith [1996] AC 155 | 95 |
| Palmer v. South Tees Health Authority [1999] Lloyd's Rep Med 151 | 94 |
| Parkinson v. St James's and Seacroft University Hospital NHS Trust [2002] QB 266 | 26-7 |
| Paton v. British Pregnancy Advisory Service Trustees [1979] QB 276 | 14 |
| Paton v. UK (1981) 3 EHRR 408 | 27 |
| Pearce v. United Bristol Healthcare NHS Trust [1999] PIQR P 53 | 47-8 |
| Peters v. Netherlands (1994) 77-ADR 75 | 61 |
| Plymouth & Torbay Health Authority and Exeter and North Devon Health Authority [1998] PIQR P 170 | 117 |
| R, *Re* (Adult: Medical Treatment) [1996] 2 FLR 99 | 110 |
| R, *Re* (Minor) (Wardship: Medical Treatment) [1991] 4 All ER 177 | 53 |
| R. v. Adomako [1995] 1 AC 171 | 152, 154, 156 |
| R. v. Bateman (1925) 19 Cr App R 8 | 153, 156 |
| R. v. Brown [1993] 2 All ER 75 | 39 |
| R. v. Burstow; R. v. Ireland [1997] 3 WLR 534 | 38 |
| R. v. Cambridge Health Authority, *ex parte* B [1995] 1 WLR 898 | 110 |
| R. v. Central Birmingham Health Authority, *ex parte* Collier (1988) unreported | 98 |
| R. v. Chief Constable of West Midlands, *ex parte* Wiley [1994] 3 WLR 433 | 80 |
| R. v. Clarence (1888) 22 QBD 23 | 37-9 |
| R. v. Department of Health, *ex parte* Source Informatics Ltd [2000] Lloyd's Rep. Med. 76 | 2-3, 74 |
| R. v. Dica [2004] EWCA Crim 1103 | 38-9 |
| R. v. G [2004] 1 AC 1034 | 155 |
| R. v. General Medical Council, *ex parte* Burke [2004] EWHC 1879 | 61-3, 65, 169-70 |
| R. v. Howe [1987] 1 AC 417 | 149 |

| | |
|---|---|
| R. v. Human Fertilisation and Embryology Authority, *ex parte* Blood [1997] 2 WLR 806 | 6 |
| R. v. K (1993) 97 Cr App Rep 342 | 81 |
| R. v. Mid Glamorgan FHSA, *ex parte* Martin [1995] 1 WLR 110 | 81, 86 |
| R. v. Misra and Srivastava [2004] EWCA Crim 2375 | 153, 156 |
| R. v. Morgan [1976] AC 182 | 39 |
| R. v. Richardson [1998] 2 Cr App R 2000 | 38 |
| R. v. Secretary of State for Health, *ex parte* Walker (1992) 3 BMLR 32 | 98 |
| R. v. Secretary of State for the Home Office, *ex parte* Benson (unreported) 1 Nov 1988 | 81 |
| R. v. Secretary of State for Social Services, *ex parte* Hincks (1992) 1 BMLR 93 | 98 |
| R. v. Wilson [1984] AC 242 | 38 |
| R. (on the application of Burke) v. General Medical Council [2004] EWHC 1879 (Admin) | 110 |
| R. (on the application of Quintavelle) v. Human Fertilisation and Embryology Authority [2004] QB 168 | 10 |
| R. (on the application of Yvonne Watts) v. (1) Bedford Primary Care Trust, (2) Secretary of State for Health [2004] Lloyd's Rep Med 113 | 109 |
| Ratcliffe | 117-19 |
| Rees v. Darlington Memorial Hospital NHS Trust [2004] 1 AC 309 | 26-7 |
| Rogers v. Whittaker (1992) 175 CLR 479 | 48 |
| Re S (Sterilisation) [2000] 2 FLR 389 | 59 |
| St George's Healthcare NHS Trust v. S [1999] Fam 36 | 59 |
| Schering Chemicals Ltd v. Falkman Ltd [1981] 2 All ER 321 | 73 |
| Shakoor v. Situ [2001] 1 WLR 410 | 112-15 |
| Sidaway v. Board of Governors of Bethlem Royal Hospital [1985] 1 AC 171; [1985] 1 All ER 643 | 35, 43-6, 48-9, 60, 65-6, 102 |
| SL, *Re* (Adult Patient) (Medical Treatment) [2000] 1 FCR 361 | 55-7 |
| Spring v. Guardian Assurance plc [1995] 2 AC 296 | 126 |

| | |
|---|---|
| *Sunday Times* v. UK [1979] 2 EHRR 245 | 154 |
| SW v. UK [1995] 21 EHRR 363 | 153 |
| Sweet v. Parsley [1970] AC 132 | 155 |
| | |
| T, *Re* (Minor) (Wardship: Medical Treatment) [1997] 1 WLR 242 | 52 |
| Taylor v. West Kent Health Authority [1997] 8 Med LR 25 | 124 |
| Tredgett v. Bexley Health Authority [1994] 5 Med LR 178 | 96 |
| | |
| U v. W (Attorney-General Intervening) [1997] 2 FLR 282 | 6 |
| | |
| Vo v. France 53924/00 [2004] 2 FCR 577 | 29-30, 32-4 |
| | |
| W (Minor) (Medical Treatment: Court's Jurisdiction) [1992] 3 Med LR 317 | 53-4 |
| W v. Egdell [1990] 1 Ch 359 | 70-2, 74 |
| Ward v. Ritz Hotel (London) [1992] PIQR 315 | 105 |
| Warner v. Commissioner of Police for the Metropolis [1969] 2 AC 256 | 153 |
| White v. Chief Constable of South Yorkshire [1998] 3 WLR 1509 | 95 |
| Wilkinson v. Broadmoor Special Hospital Authority [2002] 1 WLR 419 | 169 |
| Williams v. Star Newspaper Co Ltd (1908) 24 LTR 297 | 81 |
| Wilsher v. Essex Area Health Authority [1988] AC 1074 | 129, 132, 134 |
| | |
| X v. Austria | 61 |
| X v. Bedfordshire County Council [1995] AC 633 | 93 |
| X v. Denmark (1983) 32 DR 282 | 64 |
| X v. Netherlands | 61 |
| X v. UK (1978) 14 DR 31 | 65 |
| X v. UK (1980) (DR) | 19 27 |
| X v. Y and others [1988] 2 All ER 648 | 72-4 |
| | |
| Z v. Finland 25 EHRR 371 | 87 |

# CHAPTER 1

# LEGAL ISSUES BEFORE BIRTH

## The law of genetics

This is straightforward. There isn't any. Genetics has to borrow its law from other areas. It is therefore unsurprising that the law doesn't fit properly, looks odd, and rubs painfully in sensitive places. The law has failed to keep up with genetic advances. This is worrying, because whatever one thinks about the law which governs genetics, it matters. Everyone agrees: witness the hysteria over genetically modified crops, the almost universal horror at the idea of human reproductive cloning and the concerns about the use of DNA banks.

The problem is that genes and DNA are difficult to classify. English lawyers are tidy, conservative creatures who get upset if they cannot put concepts neatly into ancient pigeonholes. DNA confounds them. It is a physical substance; English lawyers respond to that fact by saying that it should be governed by the law of property. It also bears information; English lawyers react by saying that it should be governed by the law of confidentiality and/or intellectual property. Confidentiality and the law of property are two entirely different conceptual islands. There is little communication between them. The lawyers who practise on one island do not regard themselves as qualified to practise on the other. This has led to a dangerous incoherence in the law. The Human Genetics Commission has noted the need for legislation. The request is likely to be well down the list of any Government's legislative priorities.

## Genetic confidentiality

The general law of confidentiality is considered in detail in Chapter 3. At the heart of the common law and the codifying statutes are two notions. They do not always stand easily together. First is the idea that the conscience of the discloser is a crucial determinant of whether a breach of confidence is actionable. In *R. v. Department of Health, ex parte Source Informatics Ltd*,[1] a case about pharmacists, Simon Brown LJ said, having reviewed a number of cases:

> *"To my mind the one clear and consistent theme emerging from all these authorities is this: the confidant is placed under a duty of good faith to the confider and the touchstone by which to judge the scope of his duty and whether or not it has been fulfilled or breached is his own conscience, no more and no less. One asks, therefore, on the facts of this case: would a reasonable pharmacist's conscience be troubled by the proposed use to be made of patients' prescriptions? Would he think that by entering [the data collection agency's] scheme he was breaking his customers' confidence, making unconscientious use of the information they provide?"*[2]

In deciding what the conscience of a reasonable professional says, the courts always pay close attention to the disciplinary codes of the professional organisations. In the past the courts have tended to be more forgiving than the professional conduct committees. There are some signs that that is changing. Increasingly, a disclosing doctor will be damned by the court if he would be

---

1. [2000] Lloyd's Rep. Med. 76.
2. At 82.

damned by the GMC, and excused by the court if he would be excused by the GMC.

The other principle is that a breach of confidence will be actionable if the public interest in disclosure does not outweigh the public interest in maintaining confidence. The balancing of public interests is quintessentially a judicial activity. It presupposes an objective answer: where, objectively, does the public interest lie? That is in stark contrast to the partial subjectivity of the *Source Informatics* enquiry: "What should register in the conscience of the (admittedly reasonable) professional?" There is a lot less room for manoeuvre in the public interest balancing test than in the conscience test. Either something is in the public interest or it is not. But professionals can and very often do differ very materially but very reasonably over matters of conscience.

There are also concerns about how genetic information might be used under the provisions of the sinister s.60 of the Health and Social Care Act 2001. Section 60(1) provides that *"The Secretary of State may by regulations make such provision for and in connection with requiring or regulating the processing of prescribed patient information for medical purposes as he considers necessary or expedient – (a) in the interests of improving patient care, or (b) in the public interest."* This is potentially very scarily wide. It must be watched carefully. Lots of genetic information is thrown up incidentally in the course of routine genetic testing for specific conditions. Would regulations permitting that information to be held as part of a national database of epidemiological information about the incidence of particular damaging genetic traits be *ultra vires?* It is unlikely. And why stop at information about specific traits? Almost all genetic information is potentially medically significant. Do we really want the National Health Service, and anyone capable of hacking into its computers, to have access to information about ourselves which even we do not know? Is it ethical to hold potentially life-saving information about a patient and not disclose it? If the general answer to that question is no, what about the patient's right not to know? The creation of a national genetic database, as is proposed in Iceland, has political connotations: if the state knows more about each citizen than the citizen knows, the relation between the individual and the state has shifted significantly. What on earth does Article 8 of the ECHR have to say about all this? Some of the answers to the ECHR question have been hinted at in contexts other than genetics, and are outlined in Chapter 3.

These are big issues. For lawyers there are lots of smaller but succulent bits and pieces in the pot of genetic confidentiality. By s.170(b) of the Road Traffic Act 1988, for instance, where the driver or rider of a vehicle is alleged to be guilty of a road traffic offence, *"any other person shall if required ... give such information which it is in his power to give and may lead to the identification of the driver."* Does this require a person who is a relative of a suspected driver to undergo genetic testing in order to confirm the suspect's identity? And what about the National Health Service (Venereal Diseases) Regulations 1974, which permit disclosure of information relating to "sexually transmitted diseases" where that disclosure is necessary to prevent the spread of the disease. Genetic diseases are obviously in one sense "sexually transmitted". Do the regulations permit a doctor to trumpet abroad the information that Mr. A is the carrier of a gene for a particular disease so that his chances of passing it on are reduced? It would be a brave barrister who argued it, but the argument is not ridiculous.

**Gene therapy**

One's genes can sometimes be tinkered with so that they act in a helpful way towards disease. On its face there are no great difficulties with that. But what if (a) the process of tinkering incidentally alters your genetic make-up in a way which will be reflected in any offspring you produce; or (b) the tinkering is intended not to affect you but to alter your germ cells so as to create or eliminate characteristics in any offspring? One would have thought that the law would have at least seen the potential problems. But it appears not to have done.

## Intellectual property in genetic material

The ethics of patenting genetics and genetic information are tricky. Obvious and important questions about human dignity and autonomy arise, but have featured little in the public debate. That debate has been rather crudely pragmatic. The biotechnology companies have pointed out that the potential benefits from gene research are colossal, but that this research is extremely expensive and simply will not happen unless the fruits of research can be protected by a patent. They have also relied on the observation that isolated genes do not occur naturally, and say that, accordingly, to patent a gene is not patenting nature. Opponents of this position have tended to assert that it is offensive to make money from human body parts. The rhetorical landscape is full of slippery slopes and dubious parallels between gene sales and prostitution.

The law is summarised in Directive 98/44 EC, which has been implemented in the UK in The Patents Regulations 2000,[3] The Patents (Amendment) Rules 2001[4] and The Patents and Plant Variety Rights (Compulsory Licensing) Regulations 2002.[5] It is

---

3. SI 2000/2037.
4. SI 2001/1412.
5. SI 2002/247.

complex, and gives little comfort to conservatives. There are predictable prohibitions on the patentability of processes for cloning human beings or modifying the germ line genetic identity of human beings, and also for modifying the genetic identity of animals where that modification causes suffering and where there is no likely substantial benefit to man or animal, but, that said, the tone of the rules is very much in favour of recognising intellectual property rights in genetic products. The simple discovery of an element of the human body is not patentable, and this includes the sequence or partial sequence of a gene,[6] but the force of this is hugely diminished by the provision that *"An element isolated from the human body or otherwise produced by means of a technical process, including the sequence or partial sequence of a gene, may constitute a patentable invention, even if the structure of that element is identical to that of a natural element."*[7]

## Questions relating to the ownership of gametes

The 1990 Act has detailed provisions dealing with the use that can be made of sperm and eggs provided in the course of treatment governed by the Act. Some of the litigation about these provisions has received a lot of media coverage. The classic example is the Diane Blood case, in which the English courts found that the Act did not entitle Diane Blood to use the sperm of her dead husband because he had not given the requisite written consent for its use.[8] There was public outrage. It seemed very unfair to many. But rules were rules, said the court. The philosophy behind those rules is clear enough. Bequeathing genes to the next generation is a serious

---

6. The 2000 Regulations, Schedule A2: Regulation 3(a).
7. The 2000 Regulations, Schedule A2: Regulation 5.
8. *R. v. Human Fertilisation and Embryology Authority, ex parte Blood* [1997] 2 WLR 806; see too *U v. W (Attorney-General Intervening)* [1997] 2 FLR 282.

business. No one should be made to reproduce against his or her will. Parliament had in mind many spectres when it approved the legislation. One was of a man being confronted by a son, of whom he had no knowledge, claiming an emotional relationship. That sort of confrontation, said Parliament, was good neither for the father nor the son. Another was of a child, or its mother, seeking some sort of financial contribution from a father who never knew he was a father.

Outside the ambit of the 1990 Act, however, the position is much less clear. What happens, for example, if a woman removes semen from a condom used by her boyfriend and, knowing that he would object, inseminates herself with it? The simple answer is that we don't know. The difficulty arises from the English law's uncertainty about the ownership of body parts and body substances. This issue is returned to in Chapter 5, which deals with the title to body parts after death. Considering first the criminal law possibilities: has the girlfriend committed any criminal offence at all? Even if the law would regard the semen as capable of constituting property (and there is a big debate about that, outlined in Chapter 5), can she sensibly be said to have stolen it? Has the boyfriend not abandoned it, in a way analogous to throwing an empty bottle into a dustbin? If so, it is not "property belonging to another", within the meaning of the Theft Act, and cannot be stolen. Probably the better position is that no offence has been committed.

The position in civil law is equally uncertain. Presumably, in order for the girlfriend to have "converted" the sperm to her own use (acted with it in a way inconsistent with the rights of the owner), one would have to assert not only that there was property in the sperm (facing the same difficulties as in the criminal law definition of property, discussed above), but also that the boyfriend had a continuing proprietary right (facing the same difficulties as in the criminal law definition of abandonment, discussed above). Chapter 5 argues that the law should be more pragmatic in its definition of property and abandonment. It should assert that there is property when to fail to do so would lead to an obviously unjust result, and conclude that there is no abandonment where the abandoner would decree that the abandoned material should not be used in the way that it has been. A proprietary right, in other words, should persist for as long as (a) nobody else has acquired better title; and (b) the original title holder wishes to assert his right, for purposes in accordance with the general policy of the law.

Answers to these criminal and civil questions will be needed sooner or later. An answer to the criminal question is needed for the same policy reasons which lie behind the 1990 Act: this mishandling of gametes is obviously undesirable and needs to be discouraged. An answer to the civil question is needed because, under the existing family law, a man propelled unknowingly and unwillingly into fatherhood in the self-insemination circumstances described above might be saddled with financial liability for the child. Most people would think that this is wrong. The family legislation could be altered, but a re-draft would create some big problems of its own. It would be neater if the civil law entitled a man to bring an action for conversion of his semen – part of the damages for which would be any financial liability he shouldered under the Child Support legislation. He would no doubt want to annexe to this claim a plea for damages for breach of his right under Article 8 of the European Convention on Human Rights.

## The Human Fertilisation and Embryology Act 1990
*Introduction*

There is a raft of complex legislation which governs the artificial management of human reproduction. The main Act is the Human

Fertilisation and Embryology Act 1990. Its detailed provisions are outside the scope of this book, although one case involving the Act (the *Hashmi* case) is discussed. This case gives a good idea of the general forensic landscapes which are the battlegrounds. The Act delegates a lot of decision-making to the Human Fertilisation and Embryology Authority (HFEA). Some say that there is too much delegation, and that the HFEA is making decisions which go so fundamentally to what we perceive human beings and society to be that they should be the province of Parliament alone.

Much of the litigation about the Act has concerned its definitions of things like "embryo". The debates have been technical. The parties questioning the Authority's interpretations have been motivated by a desire to restrict the use of artificial reproduction.

The courts have generally, at least at appellate level, been supportive of the HFEA. They have resisted the attempts of moral conservatives to frustrate the general will of Parliament, expressed in the 1990 Act, which was to facilitate the use of new technology. It is perfectly true that scientific advance has run fast, and has run ahead of anything which the draftsmen of the 1990 Act could have envisaged. That has meant that the Act has sometimes creaked at the seams, and the judges have had to be more than usually purposive in their interpretation.

Broadly, the 1990 Act is liberal so far as very early, pre-implantation embryos are concerned. There are, of course, many such "spare" embryos created as the by-products of IVF procedures. The clear philosophy is that embryos at this stage cannot be regarded as quintessentially human. They can, for instance, be used for experimentation. At this stage they are composed of multi-potent stem cells – cells which have the potential to become any type of cell. Later in development, differentiation occurs: stem cells transmute into specialised cells.

At this stage the die begins to be cast at the cellular level. Potential becomes realised. And it is broadly at this stage that the 1990 Act starts to be much more jealously protective of embryos. The proponents of the Act say that this is philosophically coherent: that it has the effect of protecting human beings even in the very early stages of their march towards the individuality which the law is so keen to guard. The Act's opponents say that there is obviously individuality well before the stage of differentiation. It is inherent in the genes which each cell possesses. The fact that it is not yet expressed in differentiated cells is neither here nor there: if one purports to protect human potential, one has to protect even the one cell embryo.

This book does not seek to arbitrate. But it is perhaps pertinent to point out that if the Act really does honour human potential, lots of its sister legislation does not. It is rather vain to say that 100 cell embryos are safe in the hands of the 1990 Act if 24 week fetuses can be aborted under the Abortion Act 1967.

## "Designer embryos"
### The pre-implantation selection of desired characteristics

One example illustrates well the courts' purposive approach to the 1990 Act: the tragic case of *R. (on the application of Quintavalle) v. Human Fertilisation and Embryology Authority*.[9]

Zain Hashmi suffers from a life-threatening blood condition called beta thalassaemia. The conventional treatment for it is traumatic. His long term prognosis is uncertain but unlikely, on that conventional treatment, to be good.

Zain may be cured if he receives some stem cells from the umbilical cord of a sufficiently well tissue-matched sibling. The

---

9. [2004] QB 168.

chances of his parents producing such a tissue-matched sibling by natural means are remote. The only realistic chance of getting the cells is by the creation of embryos by IVF, removal and examination of a cell from each developing embryo, and implantation into the mother of a matched embryo. The matched embryo would then be borne to term in the usual way, and stem cells harvested at birth. The unmatched embryos would meet the fate of any "spare" embryos produced during IVF procedures: they would be stored, disposed of or used for research.

Zain's parents asked the HFEA for permission to undertake this procedure. The HFEA said yes. The pro-life campaigner Josephine Quintavalle challenged the decision by way of judicial review.

The Act prohibits creating, keeping or using an embryo except pursuant to a licence granted by the HFEA: s.3(1). The licences which the HFEA can lawfully grant are restricted by s.11. The only head of s.11 which is relevant here is s.11(1)(a), which permits the grant of *"licences under paragraph 1 of Schedule 2 of this Act authorising activities in the course of providing treatment services."* The potentially relevant part of that paragraph in Schedule 2 is (d), which allows the licensing, in the course of providing treatment services, of "practices designed to secure that embryos are in a suitable condition to be placed in a woman or to determine whether embryos are suitable for that purpose." So we have to go to the statutory definition of "treatment services". This is in s.2(1), which provides that *"'treatment services' means medical, surgical or obstetric services provided to the public or a section of the public for the purpose of assisting women to carry children."*

The real question here was whether the proposed procedure was "for the purpose of assisting women to carry children".

The judge at first instance could not agree that that was the purpose of the procedure: the embryo biopsy was not necessary to allow Mrs. Hashmi to carry children in general. There was no evidence that she could not conceive naturally, and even if she could not, embryo biopsy would not help her either to conceive or to bear a child conceived *in vitro*.

The HFEA's argument, which ultimately prevailed, was that the screening was necessary to assist Mrs. Hashmi to carry a child because her carrying a child at all was conditional on her knowing that that child was of a tissue type which could help to save Zain. No screening: no child. This was just the flip side of pre-implantation diagnosis of genetic defects. A woman might choose only to carry a child if she could be reassured that it did not have the gene for a particular disease. Parliament clearly intended to permit the pre-implantation diagnosis of defects. It would be, said the court, irrational to permit screening by way of embryo biopsy for a negative feature but not for a positive one.

The 1990 Act has shown itself to be more elastic, in sympathetic judicial hands, than many of its critics thought it was. Although there will need to be some tweaking of the legislation to cope with new reproductive technology, the root and branch revision sought by the campaigners is unlikely to occur. If it does, the prevailing political mood is very much in favour of reproductive technology, and one can imagine the Quintavalles looking wistfully back to the good old days of an accountable and fairly conservative HFEA.

**Pre-implantation diagnosis**

It is increasingly possible to identify in embryos genes which might be harmful (or beneficial). This makes it possible to select for implantation only those ones which do not have the undesired or do have the desired characteristics. This procedure is regulated by licences granted by the HFEA.[10] Although the HFEA only issues licences for the use of pre-implantation diagnosis to detect certain diseases, there is no *statutory* bar on the use of this procedure to select desirable characteristics rather than to eliminate harmful ones. There has not yet been any judicial scrutiny of the HFEA's practice in issuing licences. However, inherent in the Court of Appeal's endorsement of the HFEA's action in the *Hashmi* case was an assumption that pre-implantation diagnosis of damaging genetic conditions was lawful. In brief, England has all the legislative machinery ready to endorse positive and negative eugenics.

## Cloning

Reproductive cloning (the creation of new, born, human beings identical to a single "parent") is unlawful in the UK.[11] The inclusion of the word "born" in that definition is important, because the UK has now distinguished itself (triumphantly or shamefully, depending on your point of view), by permitting therapeutic cloning. This involves the creation of embryos (genetically, of course, fully human beings), from whom stem cells are harvested. Those stem cells are at least potentially useful in research on and treatment of some diseases. The HFEA can grant licences for such cloning.[12] Note, though, that the House of Lords Select Committee Report which ushered in therapeutic cloning stated that *"embryos should not be created specifically for*

---

10. A good overview of the procedure, and a set of guidelines, have been issued by the Genetic Commissioning Advisory Group: see http://www.doh.gov.uk/genetics/pdfs/pgdpaper.pdf.
11. See the Human Reproductive Cloning Act 2001.
12. See the Human Fertilisation and Embryology (Research) Regulations 2001 (SI No. 2001/188).

*research purposes unless there is a demonstrable and exceptional need that cannot be met by the use of surplus embryos [from IVF procedures]"*. The same logic should debar therapeutic cloning where the use of stem cells from non-embryonic sources (eg, from the umbilical cord, or, as is increasingly becoming practicable, from adults) will do. The early signs are that the HFEA is not applying these criteria rigorously.

## The rights of the fetus
### *When is a human not a human?*

The traditional position in English law has been that at the moment of expulsion from the womb a child suddenly becomes fully, legally human. It is immediately invested with the full protection of the law. Before that, though, it was nothing. *"There can be no doubt ...,"* said Sir George Baker, *"... that in England and Wales the fetus has no right of action, no right at all, until birth."*[13]

A statement this simple is bound to be wrong, and Sir George Baker was wrong. There are a number of exceptions to his general rule. Some of those exceptions are discussed below. But insofar as he was right, it is important to consider whether the reasons the English law has conventionally given to justify this position withstand analysis. That question is considered below in the context of Article 2 – protection of fetal life.

Procuring abortion has long been a common law offence. The old common law offences became statutory offences in the Offences Against the Person Act 1861. But to say that somebody could be prosecuted for killing or injuring an unborn child is rather different from saying that the unborn child has a right not to be killed or injured. One obvious difference is that in a prosecution

---

13.  *Paton v. British Pregnancy Advisory Service Trustees* [1979] QB 276 at 279.

the complaining voice would not be that of the dead child, saying that it had been violated, but the voice of the Queen, saying that she was outraged on behalf of all her subjects. The most recent judicial foray in the criminal context into the philosophically murky waters of human identity before birth concluded that the fetus was a legally anomalous thing, characterised more by its potential to be a person than any personhood which it actually possessed.[14] Harming potential was, for the House of Lords, not the same as harming an actual human being.

There are some strange inconsistencies in the law. An unborn child can be a legal person, for instance, for the purposes of succession. On the face of it this is odd. It comes from the English law's peculiar obsession with property: property tends to be regarded as more important than personal safety or even existence. So we have the Alice in Wonderland proposition that an unborn child can protest that its entitlement to Whiteacre Wood is not being respected, but may not be able to protest that it is about to be killed and washed down a sink.

Much of the law relating to the rights of the fetus has been worked out in the context of the eternal competition between the fetus and the mother. In English law the mother has consistently won. A mother, for instance, is entitled to refuse medical treatment which would save the fetus. The mother's right to autonomy trumps any right to life the fetus may have.

## The law of abortion

The classic example of this competition and that result is the Abortion Act 1967. Section 1 is worth setting out in full:

---

14. See, for example, *A-G's Reference (No. 3 of 1994)* [1996] QB 581.

*"(1) Subject to the provisions of this section, a person shall not be guilty of an offence under the law relating to abortion when a pregnancy is terminated by a registered medical practitioner if two registered medical practitioners are of the opinion, formed in good faith:*

*(a) that the pregnancy has not exceeded its twenty-fourth week and that the continuance of the pregnancy would involve risk, greater than if the pregnancy were terminated, of injury to the physical or mental health of the pregnant woman or any existing children of her family; or*

*(b) that the termination is necessary to prevent grave permanent injury to the physical or mental health of the pregnant woman; or*

*(c) that the continuance of the pregnancy would involve risk to the life of the pregnant woman, greater than if the pregnancy were terminated; or*

*(d) that there is a substantial risk that if the child were born it would suffer from such physical or mental abnormalities as to be seriously handicapped.*

*(2) In determining whether the continuance of a pregnancy would involve such risk of injury to health as mentioned in paragraph (a) or (b) of sub-section (1) of this section, account may be taken of the pregnant woman's actual or reasonably foreseeable environment."*

The huge majority of abortions are carried out under s.1(1)(a). The reality is that, despite the reassurances given to Parliament at the time the 1967 Act was passed, s.1(1)(a) gives abortion on demand up to 24 weeks of gestation. There is never any problem finding doctors who will give the s.1(1)(a) declaration simply on the basis that the woman says that she does not want to be pregnant. The counselling which is generally given before abortion is carried out is generally cursory: it is usually restricted to warnings about the possible immediate physical consequences of the procedure – vaginal bleeding and so on. There is, however, mounting evidence of more significant and lasting *sequelae* to abortion – in particular psychiatric injury and an increased risk of breast cancer. This is controversial territory, but if that evidence is reliable, it should change abortion practice in two ways. First: practitioners should not be so blithe in making the s.1(1)(a) declaration. And second: the law of consent would require practitioners to explain these risks to women seeking abortion, with the possible result that more women might decline the procedure.

The 24 week restriction applies only to s.1(1)(a). Sections 1(1)(b), (c) and (d) permit, in the specified circumstances, abortion up to term. "... grave permanent injury ...", in s.1(1)(b) is, since it includes injury to the mental health of the woman, capable of very wide interpretation. The definition of "seriously handicapped" in s.1(1)(d) has yet to be considered by the courts. It has in the past been used to justify abortion on the basis of easily remediable disabilities such as cleft lip and palate. In seems that some medical practitioners consider that a disability is serious if the woman concerned thinks that it is – a conclusion which drives a coach and horses through the originally envisaged philosophy of the Act. The Act is under-policed by the courts. The gynaecological establishment is firmly supportive of abortion, and the lawyers tend to assume that the doctors, not the courts, should be the ultimate arbiters of what is acceptable abortion practice.

*Legal problems associated with late abortion*

Late abortions require induction of labour. This occasionally leads to the live birth of a unwanted baby, and to the birth of some important and difficult legal problems. Assume that the lethal injection has failed to kill the fetus. The baby is born. On its emergence it immediately becomes entitled to the full protection of the law. It can, for instance, become a ward of court, whereas it could not *in utero*. The attending clinicians immediately acquire a duty of care towards it. If it would have been, with proper care, capable of surviving, there are no good reasons why, if it is allowed to die, its estate could not bring an action for damages against the clinicians. Similarly, it is difficult to see why death from a complete absence of medical care could not ground criminal proceedings for gross negligence manslaughter. There is no obvious difference in principle between a gynaecologist who stands by and lets a neonate die, and an anaesthetist who wanders off in the middle of an operation, allowing his patient to die. The anaesthetist would be at grave risk of prosecution.

The gynaecologist would say that since the law entitled him to kill *in utero*, accidental survival *ex utero* should not change his liability. This amounts to him saying, though, that the law does not recognise a huge legal transformation in a person as soon as it is born – a proposition which is difficult to advance on the authorities and which invites the riposte: "Fair enough: that must mean that there should be some sort of liability for intrauterine infanticide." He would no doubt seek to take refuge in some of the comments in *Bland*[15] to the effect that a doctor should not be pilloried in the criminal courts for fulfilling a duty imposed on him by the civil law. But that does not work either: there is no duty to engage in abortions. Even if there were, it would not be a duty easily comparable to the duty spoken of in *Bland* – which was simply a duty to act in the patient's best interests. Once the baby is born it

---

15. *Airedale NHS Trust v. Bland* [1993] AC 789.

becomes a patient. It will rarely be possible to argue that it was in the baby's best interests to die.

## *Suing for intrauterine damage*

Lots of medical intervention and non-intervention can harm the fetus. If a doctor, for instance, negligently prescribes a teratogenic drug to the mother, the fetus may be born without limbs. Or if, during labour, there is inadequate fetal monitoring, signs of fetal distress may be missed and the baby born with cerebral palsy. In each of these cases it would be unjust if the baby, when born, cannot sue the responsible clinicians for compensation. But, of course, the English law has traditionally had a problem about that. The old lawyers would say that if a fetus is not a legal person during its intrauterine life, it clearly cannot sue before it is born. And after it is born, it cannot sue for damages for personal injury caused at a time when it was not a person. These corollaries of the common law position are obviously absurd. The absurdity has now been swept away by the Congenital Disabilities (Civil Liability) Act 1976, which allows a fetus which has managed to be born and to survive 48 hours of extrauterine life to bring proceedings for damage caused before it was born. This statute, while redressing many obvious injustices, raises some obvious and worrying questions. Why the 48 hour survival requirement? Does this requirement not imply that the suffering of a baby which is less than two days old is not worth suing about? What if the negligence has caused the very injuries which cause the child to fail to survive 48 hours? Then the clinicians will be beneficiaries of their own incompetence – another example of the well-known maxim of cynical lawyers that it is far cheaper to kill someone than to injure them.

There is one thing that a child cannot sue for: his own

existence. He cannot go to court and say: "My life is, because of my disability, so miserable that I should never have been allowed to come into the world. The doctors are negligent for not aborting me." The courts put their reasons for this in various ways. Sometimes they presume conclusively that it is better to exist than not to exist. Sometimes they say that since, by definition, nothing can be known about non-existence, non-existence cannot be evaluated in such a way as to make it possible to say that it is better than even badly disabled existence. And sometimes they say that it is nonsensical to sue for existence, because the existence is itself a prerequisite of bringing the action. A person who does not exist cannot stand in a courtroom or brief a barrister. These sophistries cloak a clear judicial policy: the notion that even a compromised life is a life worth living. That policy took something of a knock in the conjoined twins case,[16] but is still a generally recognised principle.

Such "wrongful life" claims fail because of s.1(2) of the Congenital Disabilities (Civil Liability) Act 1976. As noted above, the 1976 Act provides that a child born alive with a personal injury can bring a claim in some circumstances. Probably the true position is that the 1976 Act is the only route of civil redress for a child born injured.[17] To qualify, the disability must result from an occurrence which falls within s.1(2), namely one which:

"(a)  affected either parent of the child in his or her ability to have a normal healthy child; or

---

16. *Re A (Children) (Conjoined Twins: Surgical Separation)* [2001] Fam. 147.
17. See Fortin J.E.S. Is the "Wrongful Life" action really dead? (1987) JSWL 306. She suggests, more imaginatively than realistically, that if there was a common law right to claim for wrongful life, the 1976 Act does not abolish it. Anyone who tried this argument on in the High Court in England would get a good hiding. Some rather arcane ECHR points could also be taken in an effort to breathe new life into wrongful life, but they have a poor prognosis.

(b) affected the mother during her pregnancy, or affected her or the child in the course of its birth, so that the child is born with disabilities *which would not otherwise have been present"* (emphasis added).

The Law Commission intended to outlaw claims for wrongful life.[18] The highlighted words are intended to implement that view. That was how s.1(2)(b) was interpreted in the main English case on the issue, *McKay v. Essex AHA*.[19] Stephenson LJ said there that s.1(2)(b) imported "the assumption that but for the occurrence giving rise to a disabled birth, the child would have been born normal and healthy, not that it would not have been born at all."[20]

*McKay* itself concerned a birth which occurred before the passing of the 1976 Act. The Court of Appeal therefore considered the common law position, and decided that the common law similarly prohibited a claim for wrongful life. There were three main reasons for this:

*(a) Public policy considerations*
The sanctity of human life was a basic principle which informed all of English law. To allow a claim like this would be to breach that principle.

*(b) The doctor owed no duty to the child to terminate its life*
Yes, abortion was legal, but it did not follow from this that there was a duty to do a legal abortion. The existence of a duty was conditioned by the public policy considerations. There is another problem in imposing on the doctor a common law duty to do or

---

18. See its report No. 60: Report on Injuries to Unborn Children, 1974, Cmnd.5709.
19. [1982] QB 1166.
20. At 1178.

advise a termination. At the time the duty was supposed to have been owed, the child was not, for these purposes, a legal person. How can one owe a duty to a non-entity?

*(c) Evaluation of the damage was impossible*
Each of the judges comments on this. One passage makes the point:

> *"The only loss for which those who have not injured the child can be held liable to compensate the child is the difference between its condition as a result of their allowing it to be born alive and injured and its condition if its embryonic life had been ended before its life in the world had begun. But how can a court evaluate that second condition and so measure the loss to the child? Even if a court were competent to decide between the conflicting views of theologians and philosophers and to assume an 'after life' or non-existence as the basis for the comparison, how can a judge put a value on one or the other, compare either alternative with the injured child's life in this world and determine that the child has lost anything, without the means of knowing what, if anything, it has gained?"*[21]

The issue of wrongful life will no doubt be revisited soon by the courts. It is likely to arise in the context of disabilities which have been actively selected for. In this context it presents a peculiar and very interesting difficulty, known to philosophers as "the non-identity problem". This is simply the problem that if it were not for the disability, which is the very thing sued for, the claimant would not exist.

Take the example of deaf parents who actively choose an embryo with genes for deafness, discarding embryos which do not

---

21. Per Stephenson LJ at 1181.

have those genes. They may have good reasons for this. They may well think that the deaf world has an intensity and an intimacy which cannot be experienced in the hearing world. They may think that they will never be able to relate properly to a hearing child, and that this will inevitably compromise a hearing child. Assume for the sake of this example (a) that the procedure has been endorsed by the HFEA, making any subsequent action against the clinicians involved very difficult; and (b) that the HFEA's decision is unimpeachable. A child is duly born deaf. He brings an action against his parents, framed in the traditional "wrongful life" way, saying: "Because of my deafness my life is miserable. It would have been better if I had never been born."

On the basis of the original 1976 Act and *McKay*, probably the deaf child in the hypothetical case has no claim against the parents. The fact that the child was selected for its disabilities does not distinguish it from a child whose disabilities were not recognised or not acted on. In order to get to court to complain of its injuries, the child would have to complain of the very thing (its selection) which was a prerequisite of it being in court in the first place. It would have to un-wish itself. The court would be wandering in a forensic Wonderland. The child would have to say: "I'm here to complain about being here," and although the courts are not very philosophically sophisticated, they would think that that smelt bad.

But there is another twist. Section 1A of the 1976 Act (a later addition), provides:

> *"... in any case where:*
> *(a) a child carried by a woman as the result of the placing in her of an embryo or of sperm and eggs or her artificial insemination is born disabled,*
> *(b) the disability results from an act or omission in the course of the selection, or the keeping or use outside the body, of the embryo carried by her or of the gametes used to bring*

> *about the creation of the embryo, and*
> *(c) a person is under this section answerable to the child in respect of the act or omission, the child's disabilities are to be disregarded as damage resulting from the wrongful act of that person and actionable accordingly at the suit of the child."*

It is clear what this section is aimed at. It is meant to extend the general provisions of the 1976 Act to torts committed in the course of the exotic manipulations of reproductive technology. There has been speculation about whether the words "in the course of the selection" in sub-section (b) effectively create a right of action for wrongful life where there has been something wrong in the selection. If this is right, the choice of the deaf couple could be an "act" which, if deemed to be wrong, could entitle the child to damages for being born.[22] But the courts are unlikely to agree with this construction, for three main reasons. First, the more natural reading of the section suggests that it is aimed at torts committed during the course of the selection, rather than at the selection itself. Second, the legislative history of the section suggests this too. A cause of action as ethically tricky as wrongful life is unlikely to have slipped unnoticed into the statute book. Nobody suggested at the time that this sub-section was being debated that this would be its effect. Third, this reading has all the fundamental difficulties identified in *McKay*.

## Actions by parents for "wrongful birth"

It is common for children to be born as a result of medical

---

22. This is argued by Kennedy and Grubb in *Medical Law, Text and Materials*, Second Edition, Butterworths, at 977.

negligence. Classic examples include negligently performed sterilisation, failure to warn about the risk of failure of sterilisation, failure to perform an abortion properly, and failure to detect a fetal abnormality which, if detected, would have resulted in abortion. Circumstances like this led to a big industry of "wrongful birth" claims, in which the parents would go to court seeking compensation for the pain and suffering caused by a birth which would otherwise have been avoided, and, more importantly, for the costs of bringing up the child.[23] Those costs could sometimes be very large. They varied according to the social and financial circumstances of the parents. A family which sent their unwanted child to a boarding school could claim the fees as a consequence of the negligence. It was much cheaper to bring negligently into the world a working class child whose parents would never have dreamt of sending him to Eton.

There was something distasteful about all this. The lay response was commonly: "A child is a blessing," and "What would the child think if he found that his parents had brought High Court proceedings in which they said that they wished he had been aborted?" Others said that if a child was genuinely unwanted then the parents should be compensated, but otherwise the joy of the child should be deemed to be compensation enough. This latter answer was obviously flawed: it had the consequence, disastrous on public policy grounds, of providing a financial disincentive to love (or at least to express one's love of) one's children.

These were the considerations which compelled the House of Lords, in *McFarlane v. Tayside Health Board*,[24] to outlaw actions for the financial consequences of wrongful birth. All that a mother

---

23. The cornerstone case was *Emeh v. Kensington and Chelsea and Westminster Area Health Authority* [1985] QB 1012.
24. [2000] AC 59.

could get were damages representing the pain and suffering associated with the pregnancy and birth. The reasons were expressed in many legal ways, but what it all amounted to was that a child should be presumed to be a blessing which outweighed, or at least cancelled out, the financial and other detriments which are part of the parentage package.

There has been a flurry of subsequent litigation, probing the boundaries of *McFarlane*. Two obvious questions remained: What about disabled children? And what about disabled parents?

The case of a disabled child arose in *Parkinson v. St. James's and Seacroft University Hospital NHS Trust*.[25] The parents said that *McFarlane* could be distinguished. A disabled child could not be deemed to be a blessing as a normal one could, and, even if the policy which drove *McFarlane* made that argument illegitimate, the parents were surely entitled to receive damages representing the additional costs of bringing up a disabled child. This latter argument was adopted by the Court of Appeal, in terms which indicated the Court's dissatisfaction with what the House of Lords had said in *McFarlane*.

The House had a second opportunity to consider its own decision in *MacFarlane* in *Rees v. Darlington Memorial Hospital NHS Trust*.[26] This concerned the second question: what about a disabled parent who, as a result of her disability, will incur costs greater than those of a normal parent in bringing up the unwanted child? The reasoning in *McFarlane*, said the House, applied equally to this situation. There could be no truly compensatory damages for the additional financial liability, although, curiously, there was a £15,000 "conventional award" to the mother for all her bother. Whether this is truly compensatory is a matter of real but

---

25. [2002] QB 266.
26. [2004] 1 AC 309.

pretty sterile debate. Most of the members of the seven judge panel in *Rees* were coy about the fate of *Parkinson*: *Rees* and *Parkinson* do not sit easily together.

## The ECHR and the fetus

Many hoped that the European Convention on Human Rights would iron out many of the absurdities in the law relating to the fetus; that it would act like a sort of forensic mortar, bridging the gaps between the disparate areas of relevant law and welding it into a coherent whole. So far, though, the Convention has disappointed.

There is considerable confusion about whether Article 2 (and, by extension, Articles 3 and 8) can protect the fetus. The possibility that Article 2 might apply to the fetus was not ruled out by the Commission in *H v. Norway*,[27] but the facts of that case give few grounds for fetal comfort. A 14 week fetus was aborted on the grounds, legal in Norway, that "pregnancy, birth or care for the child may place the woman in a difficult situation of life" – a provision analogous to s.1(1)(a) of the English Act of 1967. Those provisions were held to be Article 2 compliant. In other words, any application of Article 2 to the fetus (it not being admitted that there is any such application) must be restricted by consideration of the mother's competing claims. The Commission relied expressly on this feto-maternal competition in its decision in *Paton v. United Kingdom*.[28] It said that to assert an absolute right to fetal life under Article 2 might endanger the mother's life: it might have the effect

---

27. (1992) 73 DR 155. See too *X v. UK* (1980) (DR) 19; *H v. Norway* (1992) DR 73 and *Boso v. Italy* (2002) No. 50490/99, in which the court, considering abortion, admitted the possibility that the fetus might have an Article 2 right, but would not say that it did.
28. (1981) 3 EHRR 408.

of preferring the life of the unborn child to that of the mother. That, the Commission said, could not be right, and accordingly if the fetus had any Article 2 right, it must be qualified by reference to maternal interests.

As an abstract proposition this seems logical enough. If one has to choose between two lives, it is reasonable to opt for the mother's. It seems correct that the absolute nature of Article 2 should not have the ironic effect of depriving the mother of the protection which Article 2 is designed to give. But if one acknowledges that the notion of a competition between the interests of the mother and the interests of the fetus is a valid analytical tool, one must be prepared to weigh those competing interests. If in one pan of the scales one has the life of the fetus, and in the other one has, not the death or serious injury of the mother but her social convenience, where should the balance lie? Can Article 2 really be said to be honoured at all if convenience wins over life?

In reality, most battles between the fetus and the mother are best described as battles between the fetus's Article 2 and Article 3 rights and the mother's Article 8 rights. In other areas of human life that contest should be and is an entirely one-sided one: Article 2 and Article 3 should win every time. But the legal referees seem to have a blind spot when it comes to this particular dispute.

The easy way off the horns of this dilemma is simply to say that Article 2 should not apply to fetal life at all. But that itself would be an odd result. It would entail saying (for example) that a 40 week fetus which had simply not been expelled from the uterus, but would be perfectly capable of medically unsupported life if it were expelled, should have no right to life (or, presumably, other basic rights); whereas a fetus which, by medical accident or design had been born prematurely and required intensive maintenance should have (as it uncontroversially does) all the basic rights. That elevates the arbitrary moment of birth to a significance which science suggests it should not have.

Is was widely hoped that the judgement of the ECtHR in *Vo v. France* would indicate, once and for all, the extent of the protection given by the Convention to the fetus. But those hopes were dashed.[29] It was billed as the cornerstone judgment on the application of Article 2 of the ECHR to the human embryo and fetus. And, indeed, it is an important judgment. It is the ultimate masterpiece of Strasbourgeois equivocation; the clearest possible indication that Strasbourg will refuse to grasp the nettle in difficult cases; an illustration of the fact that, in the jurisprudence of the Strasbourg court, philosophically tricky problems can just be flushed down the forensic toilet which lawyers call the "margin of appreciation."

The facts were simple and tragic. In 1991 two women, both called Mrs. Vo, went at the same time to the Lyons General Hospital. The Mrs. Vo who was to become the applicant in these proceedings was six months pregnant. She wanted the baby very much. The other Mrs. Vo was due to have a coil removed. There was a mix-up. The applicant was called in to have her non-existent coil removed. The doctor did not examine her before trying to remove it. He pierced the amniotic sac. This meant that the pregnancy could not continue, and a termination was duly carried out.

The applicant was distraught. She pursued the doctor through the French courts. She had some successes, but finally the Court of Cassation concluded that the doctor was not guilty of unintentional homicide. The applicant went to Strasbourg, saying that if the offence of unintentional homicide did not apply to the death of an

---

29. 53924/00: [2004] 2 FCR 577: see the website: www.echr.coe.int/Eng/Judgments.htm.

unborn child, the State had failed to discharge its obligations under Article 2.

The Government said, first, that Article 2 did not apply to the unborn child, and, second, that there was an adequate domestic remedy apart from a criminal sanction – namely an action for damages. The first of those submissions is the interesting and fundamental one.

The relevant part of Article 2 of course provides that: "Everyone's right to life shall be protected by law ..." The central point was: Does "everyone" (*"toute personne"* in French) include an unborn child?

The existing case-law of the Strasbourg court made it possible for both sides to claim the jurisprudential high ground. In *Vo* the court rather overstated the effect of the previous cases by saying: *"... in the circumstances examined to date by the Convention institutions – that is, in the various laws on abortion – the unborn child is not regarded as a 'person' directly protected by Article 2 ... and that if the unborn do have a 'right' to 'life' it is implicitly limited by the mother's rights and interests. The Convention institutions have not, however, ruled out the possibility that in certain circumstances safeguards may be extended to the unborn child ..."*

The applicant said that, as a matter of scientific fact, life began at conception. An unborn child at any stage of gestation could not be regarded as either a cluster of cells or an object. It was quintessentially human (all the more so if it would have been capable of life outside the uterus). It had, in the past, been regarded as legally convenient for some purposes to invest humans with legal personality as soon as they were expelled from the uterus, but that view was an unbiological archaism. The only modern way of interpreting *"toute personne"* in Article 2 was to regard it as meaning human beings rather than individuals who possessed the artificial attribute of legal personality. Pressing the argument perhaps rather counter-productively far, she asserted that this interpretation of Article 2 should outlaw all forms of abortion, with the exception of therapeutic abortion. This may have been a serious tactical blunder. The strength of this case, from the applicant's point of view, was that this was an involuntary abortion: none of the delicate business of balancing the mother's wishes against the fetus's interests, arose here.

The Government seized on this assertion eagerly. The Government agreed with the applicant's logic: if Article 2 applied to the fetus, of course it followed that abortion was contrary to Article 2. But abortion had been expressly endorsed by the court. One could therefore infer from all the abortion decisions that Article 2 could not have the effect contended for by the applicant. This was unsurprising. Neither metaphysics or medicine had given a definitive answer to the question of when human life began: how then could the court, which had to reflect the different philosophical traditions of the various Convention signatories, do any better? It went on to say that if the Convention had intended to apply to the fetus, it would have said so. The other rights protected by the Convention, anyway, applied to post-natal people. It would be strange if one could be a person for the purposes of Article 2, but not for the other Articles. Consistency therefore demanded that the fetus did not fall within the ambit of Article 2.

This was a judgment of the Grand Chamber. There were 17 judges. Fourteen of them held that there had been no violation of Article 2, and there were three blistering dissents.

The court reviewed in detail the various international declarations there have been which deal with the rights of the unborn child. There are many of these, including the Orviedo Convention on Human Rights and Biomedicine (with its additional protocols on biomedical research and on the prohibition of cloning), the report of the Working Party on the Protection of the Human Embryo and Fetus, and the opinion of the EC European Group on Ethics in Science and New Technologies. None of these deals squarely with the issue of the time from which human embryos ought to be treated as legally equivalent to post-natal humans. Their failure appeared to the court to be a ground for not grappling with the issue in the case of *Vo*. One might have thought that the lead of the court was needed precisely because no definitive lead could be found elsewhere. If a question comes to court for determination precisely because the question is difficult, it is curious for the court to refuse to answer it on the grounds that it is too difficult. The court observed that:

> "... at European level ... there is no consensus on the nature and status of the embryo and/or fetus ... although they are beginning to receive some protection in the light of scientific progress and the potential consequences of research into genetic engineering, medically assisted reproduction or embryo experimentation. At best, it may be regarded as common ground between States that the embryo/fetus belongs to the human race. The potentiality of that being and its capacity to become a person – enjoying protection under the civil law ... require protection in the name of human dignity, without making it a 'person' with the 'right to life' for the purposes of Article 2 ... Having regard to the foregoing, the Court is convinced that it is neither desirable, nor even possible as matters stand, to answer in the abstract the question whether the unborn child is a person for the purposes of Article 2 ... "

How should that undesirability or impossibility be framed in the legal language of Strasbourg? By using the ultimate refuge of the indecisive – the "margin of appreciation":

> "... the issue of when the right to life begins comes within the margin of appreciation which the Court generally considers that States should enjoy in this sphere, notwithstanding an evolutive interpretation of the Convention ... The reasons for that conclusion are, firstly, that the issue of such protection has not been resolved within the majority of the Contracting States themselves ... and, secondly, that there is no European consensus on the scientific and legal definition of the beginning of life."

It went on to say that even assuming Article 2 was applicable, on the facts, France had not failed to comply with the obligations which Article 2 would impose.

There are grave difficulties with this judgment. The main one is the refusal of the court to answer the question that it was being asked. Two of the dissenting judges were disgusted by that abdication of responsibility. They pointed out that judges are there to judge:

> "Does the present inability of ethics to reach a consensus on what is a person and who is entitled to the right to life prevent the law from defining these terms? I think not. It is the task of lawyers, and in particular judges, especially human-rights judges, to identify those notions ... that correspond to the words or expressions in the relevant legal instruments ... Why should the Court not deal with the terms 'everyone' and 'the right to life' (which the European Convention does not define) in the same way it has done from its inception with the terms 'civil rights and obligations', 'criminal charges' and 'tribunals', even if we are here concerned with philosophical, not technical, concepts."

The second, and perhaps most worrying, difficulty is the way in which, having decided to dodge the issue, the court dodged it. It invoked the idea of the margin of appreciation. That idea has a legitimate place in the construction of several Articles, but how can it relate at all to the most fundamental and absolute Article of all, Article 2? With Article 2, to dilute is to abolish. Another of the dissenting judges agreed:

> "There can be no margin of appreciation on the issue of the applicability of Article 2. A margin of appreciation may, in my opinion, exist to determine the measures that should be taken to discharge the positive obligation that arises because Article 2 is applicable, but it is not possible to restrict the applicability of Article 2 by reference to a margin of appreciation. The question of the interpretation or applicability of Article 2 (an absolute right) cannot depend on a margin of appreciation. If Article 2 is applicable, any margin of appreciation will be confined to the effect thereof."

It is tempting to say that, having read *Vo*, we are none the wiser. But we are. We know that the Convention cannot be relied upon in areas of biomedical controversy. That makes it all the more important to get our domestic legislation right.

A postscript: The Court itself noted that the Orviedo Convention on Human Rights and Biomedicine and its various protocols do not attempt a definition of the terms "everyone" or "human being". The Strasbourg court can be asked, however, under Article 29 of the Oviedo Convention, to give advisory opinions on the interpretation of that Convention. That might well be the way in which Strasbourg will have to be forced to do its job in relation to construction of these crucial terms.

# CHAPTER 2

# CONSENT

**Introduction**

The law is, in theory, very keen on human autonomy. The courts trumpet that a patient's right to make decisions about what he does with his own body is "... a basic human right protected by the common law."[1] It is protected too by the European Convention on Human Rights. You are better protected, though, if you do not need protecting. If you are a mental defective or a woman with a needle phobia you will find the courts less dewy-eyed about basic human values and much more stoutly paternalistic.

The English law is jealously protective of the Englishman's historic right to be self-endangeringly eccentric. The judges have repeatedly said that one cannot infer legal incompetence simply from the fact that the patient's decision about treatment is suicidally stupid. The following extracts from judgments illustrate this:

> "*The patient is entitled to reject [the] advice for reasons which are rational, or irrational, or for no reason.*"[2]

> "*It is established that the principle of self-determination requires that respect must be given to the wishes of the patient, so that, if an adult patient of sound mind refuses, however unreasonably, to consent to treatment or care by which his life would or might be prolonged, the doctors responsible for his*

---

1. Per Lord Scarman in *Sidaway v. Board of Governors of Bethlem Royal Hospital* [1985] 1 AC 171.
2. Per Lord Templeman in *Sidaway, supra.*

*care must give effect to his wishes, even ... though they do not consider it to be in his best interests to do so ...* "[3]

Thus medical and surgical treatment of a competent adult is unlawful unless that adult consents. Special provisions apply to minors and to others deemed incapable of giving or withholding valid consent.

One of the constant moans from doctors accused of doing a procedure without the appropriate consent is: "I acted in good faith" or "The procedure was beneficial". Neither is a defence.

**The legal consequences of failing to obtain consent**

There are three possibilities:

- criminal proceedings
- civil proceedings
- disciplinary proceedings

These are considered in turn.

**Criminal proceedings**

A doctor who does something without his patient's consent is at risk of prosecution. The commonest examples which the courts see are:

- sexual molestation:
  often when a doctor performs, for his own sexual gratification, a breast or vaginal examination for which there is no clinical justification

---

3. Per Lord Goff in *Airedale NHS Trust v. Bland* [1993] AC 789.

- unnecessary treatment for financial gain:
  such as when a dentist does fillings which the patient does not need.

One might think that it is easy to know when, in circumstances like this, a patient has given consent. But the law does not always accord with common sense. For over a century the law was dogged by a case called *R. v. Clarence*.[4] Clarence had gonorrhoea, and knew it. His wife did not know of his infection. He slept with her, and she got infected. He was prosecuted under ss.47 and 20 of the Offences Against the Person Act 1861 – causing actual (s.47) and grievous (s.20) bodily harm. At the time (the law has since changed) it was thought necessary to establish an assault, and consent is of course a defence to assault. He said that his wife had consented to the act of sexual intercourse, which indeed she had. The prosecution rejoined that there had been no true consent; that if she had been told about his infection (a fact clearly material to the decision whether or not to sleep with someone), she would have withheld her consent. Clarence was convicted. He appealed. The appeal court allowed his appeal, saying that valid consent was consent to an act of the "nature and quality" of that which was done. Mrs. Clarence had consented to an act of the "nature and quality" of that which was done – namely sexual intercourse. She knew perfectly well what sexual intercourse was, and had said yes to it.

This decision had some strange results in medical law. For example:

- a dentist suspended from practice performed dental procedures on patients who assumed that he was properly registered. They

---

4. (1888) 22 QBD 23.

said that they would not have consented had they known about the suspension. The dentist's conviction for assault occasioning actual body harm was quashed, the Court of Appeal saying that there was nothing tantamount to a mistake of identity, and that the patients knew perfectly the nature and quality of the acts they were subjected to.[5]

- a doctor inserted an instrument into a woman's vagina. He was motivated only by a desire for sexual gratification. The woman consented because she thought it was diagnostically justified. The Supreme Court of Victoria held that there was no assault: there was no fraud as to the nature and quality of the act.[6]

Ever since its promulgation, *Clarence* has had academic obloquy poured over it. The main objection was the obvious one: sexual intercourse with an infected person is not an act of the same nature and quality as sexual intercourse with an uninfected one. That is particularly obviously so when the disease concerned is a dangerous one such as HIV. There is now another objection. Assault is no longer an element of s.47 or s.20.[7] Why then should consent be a defence?

Those, more or less, were the arguments which ushered *Clarence* into legal history. Mohammed Dica was HIV positive. He had unprotected sexual intercourse with two women. The women did not know that he was HIV positive, and said that they would not have slept with him if they had known. Both became HIV positive themselves. Dica was convicted by a jury of causing grievous bodily harm. He appealed. The Court of Appeal said that

---

5. *R. v. Richardson* [1998] 2 Cr.App. R 2000.
6. *Mobilio* [1991] 1 VR 339.
7. *R. v. Wilson* [1984] AC 242: see too *R. v. Burstow; R. v. Ireland* [1997] 3 WLR 534.

*Clarence* was no longer good law, at least in the context of sexually transmitted disease. There was no true consent here. There was also some interesting discussion about the extent to which one can consent at all to serious bodily injury. While noting the general principle that one could not consent to such serious injury, the court was not impressed with the submission that simply because there was a known risk of serious injury in many acts of consenting sexual intercourse, that intercourse was unlawful. To extrapolate the general principle so that it had that conclusion would be to interfere more significantly than the judges could properly do with personal autonomy. Where there was true consent, only Parliament could write the laws of the bedroom.[8]

The implications of *Dica* still have to be worked out. It seems that it has imported into the English criminal law the idea of informed consent – the idea that consent is only valid if it is given after provision of all the information relevant to a responsible decision.

In the case of assault, a genuine but objectively unreasonable belief that consent has been granted will exculpate.[9] Recklessness will not land a doctor in prison; it might well land him in front of the GMC.

The criminal law contains an important exception to the general principle that you can consent to whatever you want. It has been mentioned already in the discussion of *R. v. Dica*. Public policy decrees that you cannot consent to really serious bodily injury. Thus if you nail someone's genitals to a piece of plywood at his express invitation, the fact of the invitation will not save you from prison.[10] The limits of this prohibition have not been explored

---

8. [2004] EWCA Crim 1103.
9. *R. v. Morgan* [1976] AC 182.
10. *R. v. Brown* [1993] 2 All ER 75.

in a medical context. Lots of surgical procedures inevitably cause serious injury: splitting open someone's chest in the course of a thoracotomy, for instance, is certainly serious injury. If a surgeon who believes that there is no therapeutic justification for an exploratory thoracotomy is talked into doing the procedure by an obsessive hypochondriac who believes that he has lung cancer, it seems at least arguable that the surgeon might be criminally liable.

## Civil proceedings

There are two broad ways in which civil proceedings based on lack of consent can be framed: trespass to the person and negligence.

## Trespass to the person

The tort usually spoken of here is battery. This is the intentional application of unlawful force to a person.

The intention here is not to do a wrong, but simply intention to do the relevant act. Again, good faith is irrelevant. The classic illustration is the Canadian case of *Malette v. Shulman*.[11]

Mrs. Malette was a Jehovah's Witness. She was badly injured. She was taken to hospital. The treating clinician, Dr. Shulman, knew that she carried a card saying that she did not want a blood transfusion. Blood was necessary to save her life, and Dr. Shulman ordered that she be given it. She lived. Instead of giving Dr. Shulman a bottle of whisky, she gave him a writ, saying that she was entitled to damages for battery. There was no defence.

A similar, well publicised English example is the case of Miss B.[12] She was paralysed from the neck down, and so all her

---

11. (1990) 67 DLR (4th) 321.
12. *B v. An NHS Trust* [2002] 2 All ER 449.

breathing was done for her by a ventilator. She wanted to die, and asked her treating clinicians to switch the ventilator off. They liked her, wanted her to live, and refused. She went to court, and the court found that she was competent. Accordingly, the unwanted treatment amounted to an assault which should be compensated for in damages.

Battery has some technical advantages for a claimant over the tort of negligence. The first is that in battery, unlike in negligence, no damage need be proved in order for the tort to be complete. If it is established that the defendant applied unlawful force, the claimant is entitled to damages, even if he is entirely uninjured. Or, put more kindly, damage is assumed.

The second advantage relates to the measure of damages. Damages in the tort of negligence are narrowly compensatory, and that compensation does not normally take into account the mental distress which is caused by the motivation of the defendant. But if battery is established there is the possibility of aggravated damages – damages representing precisely that additional outrage which comes from feeling that one has been exploited. It used to be thought that aggravated damages had a punitive element. That is clearly no longer the case, if indeed it ever was, but the categories of conduct which commonly attract aggravated damages make it clear that such damages are vehicles for expression of judicial opprobrium.

That said, the judges frown on the use of battery in a medical context. The classical frown is that of Bristow J in *Chatterton v. Gerson.*[13]

> "... it would be very much against the interests of justice if actions which are really based on a failure by the doctor to

---

13. [1981] QB 432 at 443.

*perform his duty adequately to inform were pleaded in trespass."*

That is, though, an expression of regret about the state of the law, rather than a statement of what the law is.

It is, rightly, easier to avoid liability for battery than for negligence. If the doctor gives a broad-brush sketch of what he proposes, and the patient consents, the law of trespass will regard that consent as real.[14] The law of negligence might require finer brush-strokes.[15]

A good modern example of battery in its natural legal habitat is the dental negligence case: *Appleton v. Garrett*.[16] The defendant dentist did lots of unnecessary work on several patients to enrich himself. No valid consent for that work had been given. Battery was therefore established, and the patients were found to be entitled to aggravated damages representing an additional 25 per cent of their purely compensatory damages.

**Negligence**

A typical negligence action involving consent will occur when a surgeon, in his pre-operative counselling, fails to tell the patient about the risk of a particular complication. The patient, in ignorance, gives his consent to the procedure. The complication occurs. The patient then sues the surgeon, saying that if he had

---

14. In *Chatterton v. Gerson, supra*, Bristow J said: *"Once a patient is informed in broad terms of the nature of the procedure which is intended, and gives her consent, that consent is real, and the cause of action on which to base a claim for failure to go into risks and implications is negligence, not trespass."* See also *Davis v. Barking, Havering and Brentwood HA* [1993] 4 Med LR 85.
15. See *Chatterton v. Gerson, supra*.
16. [1997] 8 Med LR 75.

known of the risk he would not have consented to the surgery. The measure of damages in such a case would be that representing compensation for the complication.

But it is not always as simple as that, as will become clear.

The cornerstone authority is the House of Lords case of *Sidaway*.[17] There is a lot of academic discussion about what *Sidaway* actually decides, but broadly it says:

(a) that the *Bolam* test applies to determination of liability. A doctor will escape liability if the pre-operative counselling he has given would be endorsed by a responsible body of medical opinion in the relevant specialty; and
(b) there will be cases where it is so blindingly obvious that a warning should have been given that, notwithstanding expert support for non-warning, the judges are perfectly capable of making up their own minds.

Proposition (b) used to be regarded by some as inconsistent with (a), but it is not at all. All it is saying (as discussed in the section on *Bolitho v. City and Hackney Health Authority:* Chapter 4), is that there are some cases which clearly demand a warning, and if any expert disagrees, he is simply not representing a *responsible* body of medical opinion. Since the judges are the ultimate arbiters of what amounts to 'responsible' (helped, of course, and usually helped definitively by medical experts), this analysis honours *Bolam* rather than breaching it.

In the realm of consent to treatment the judges have been much more ready than in other areas of clinical negligence to substitute their own opinions about what amounts to responsible practice for those of experts. This is unsurprising and logical. Judges are patients and potential patients. They know very well the sort of

---

17. *Supra.*

things which they would want to know about if they were making a decision about surgery, and how various pieces of information would be likely to affect them. Whether a particular piece of information would be likely to affect decision-making is relevant to the question of whether that piece of information should be disclosed.

So far, so good. From now on, though, the plot thickens alarmingly.

Lord Browne-Wilkinson, who gave the only substantial speech in *Bolitho*, re-asserted the relevance of the *Bolam* test in cases of "diagnosis and treatment". He said, without explaining himself further, or referring to *Sidaway* at all, that he was not there considering questions of "disclosure of risk".

Perhaps he had in mind, in inserting this mysterious caveat, the Senate of Surgery's document *"The Surgeon's Duty of Care"* (1997). It was subtitled *"Guidance for surgeons on ethical and legal issues"*. There is no doubt that was authoritative. It was published by the Senate of Surgery of Great Britain and Ireland, an umbrella organisation representing all the Royal Surgical Colleges and all the specialist surgical organisations.

The document is now of mainly historical interest because, as discussed below, it has been overtaken by the GMC's own guidelines. But it was important. It was the bridgehead from the USA to the UK of the doctrine of informed consent. It adopted a particular test for determining whether advice about risk is acceptable - the so-called "reasonable patient" test. It then put on the surgeon a further duty to determine whether, in the circumstances of an individual patient, a more detailed discussion would be required than the "reasonable patient" would demand, and if he decided that the patient needed this, to give it. There is further a duty, said the document, for surgeons to satisfy themselves that a patient's choice is the result of understanding of and deliberation about the information provided.

Up until the publication of the Senate's document there was, courtesy of *Sidaway*, no formal doctrine of informed consent in the American sense in the English law. The Senate's authoritative statement imported that doctrine to these shores. The Senate, perhaps unwittingly, took from the surgeons it represents the protection which *Sidaway* gave them. It will be no good saying that not everyone accepts this document as authoritative. The courts will readily find that all *responsible* surgeons accept it.

The GMC followed the surgeons. In November 1998 it published its new guidelines on consent entitled *"Seeking patients' consent: the ethical considerations"*.[18] These guidelines do for all medical practitioners what the Senate of Surgery did for surgeons.

They say, apparently unconscious of the irony: *"... you are expected to be aware of the legal principles set by relevant case-law in this area. Existing case-law gives a guide as to what can be considered minimum requirements of good practice in seeking informed consent from patients."* Well, not now it doesn't. If a body as authoritative as the GMC says that pre-procedure counselling and the adequacy of patient understanding has to be assessed in a certain way, the courts will be unable to say that responsible doctors would do things in a different way.

The guidelines seem at first blush eminently common sensical. Look at them closely and absurdities come crawling out. They state, for instance: *"When providing information you must do your best to find out about patients' individual needs and priorities. For example, patients' beliefs, culture, occupation or other factors may have a bearing on the information they need in order to reach a decision. You should not make assumptions about patients' views, but discuss these matters with them, and ask them whether they*

---

18. See www.gmc-uk.org/standards.

*have any concerns about the treatment or the risks it may involve. You should provide patients with appropriate information which should include an explanation of any risks to which they may attach particular significance. Ask patients whether they have understood the information and whether they would like more before making a decision."* So, there is a duty to find out what an individual patient wants to know, a duty to tell the patient that and, further and more frighteningly, a duty to ensure that that individual patient has actually understood. The difficulties are not merely practical clinical difficulties (how on earth to find the time to take the psychological and cultural inside leg measurements of patients in order to provide this bespoke consenting service), but fundamental legal difficulties too. Under *Sidaway* a doctor who, it is said, should have told a patient about a ridiculously small risk of a small complication would be able to say: "There is a responsible body of medical opinion which would not have given that warning." Under the new guidelines a patient will be able to say: "The risk you should have warned about might not have been sufficiently large or of such a nature to dissuade most, or even any other, people from the procedure. But I wanted to know about it for personal reasons, and you should have found out that I wanted to know and told me." And it will be difficult, given the way the guidelines are framed, to contradict that patient. Hopefully, the courts will impose their own notions of reasonableness when considering how diligent the enquiries should be, and it may be that *Sidaway* will live mistily on in an anomalous no-man's land between *Bolam* and naked common law reasonableness, but the fact remains that the burden of enquiry and explanation on the doctor is greater than it ever has been, and is potentially crushing.

The guidelines' overreaction is exemplified well by what they say about patients who say that they do not want themselves to know about the treatment. They assert: *"No-one may make decisions on behalf of a competent adult. If patients ask you to withhold information and make decisions on their behalf, or nominate a relative or third party to make decisions for them, you should explain the importance of them knowing the options open to them, and what the treatment they may receive will involve. If they insist they do not want to know in detail about their condition and its treatment, you should still provide basic information about the treatment ..."* This is clearly internally contradictory. What it comes to is that no-one can take a decision on behalf of a patient except the patient, unless the patient's decision is that he does not want to know, and wishes the decision about treatment to be made for him. The patient, under these rules, has no right not to know, however unnecessarily distressing knowledge may be. The rules trumpet that the patient's right is paramount: in fact that right is subservient to the apparent need of the GMC to placate the press by ensuring that everything is said regardless of the good of the patient.

The influence of Wisheart *et al* is everywhere in the rules. They provide expressly for the disclosure of clinical audit materials to questioning patients by saying: *"Some patients may want to know whether any of the risks or benefits of treatment are affected by the choice of institution or doctor providing the care. You must answer such questions as fully, accurately and objectively as possible."* Fair enough, perhaps, but where is the explanation to stop? With a critical bedside evaluation of the statistical methods used to assess the data? Many say that patients' peace of mind was best served by allowing doctors to exercise their own judgment about what to tell each patient, and only holding doctors liable where what they have done would not be endorsed by a responsible body of their professional peers.

The courts have not yet grappled with the effect of these guidelines. In *Pearce v. United Bristol Healthcare NHS Trust* the

Court of Appeal said that *"... if there is a significant risk which would affect the judgment of a reasonable patient, then in the normal course it is the responsibility of a doctor to inform the patient of that significant risk, if the information is needed so that the patient can determine for him or herself as to (sic) what course he or she should adopt."*[19]

Some commentators got excited about this, saying that it changes dramatically the legal landscape so far as consent is concerned, and noting that Lord Woolf's test does not differ materially from that of the High Court of Australia in the notorious case of *Rogers v. Whittaker*.[20] The excitement is unwarranted. *Pearce* reaffirms the traditional construction of *Sidaway*,[21] and in the passage cited simply articulates common legal and medical sense. No responsible body of medical opinion is likely to disagree with so vague and bland a formulation of general principle. *Sidaway* survives, so far as the courts are concerned, but the guidelines have made it technically otiose.

**Disciplinary jurisdiction**

The GMC takes consent issues very seriously. It has issued a number of guidelines, some of which have been referred to above. Some of the most notorious GMC disciplinary hearings have involved a failure to obtain proper consent. The best example is the Wisheart debacle; the GMC's inquiry into the Bristol paediatric cardiac surgeons.

GMC proceedings are, of course, framed loosely in terms of failing to follow the GMC's own guidelines. The guidelines are

---

19. [1999] PIQR P 53.
20. (1992) 175 CLR 479.
21. See Woolf MR at 59.

broad. They allow the Professional Conduct Committee to take action on the basis of an ethical smell, but broadly the principles to be applied in deciding whether there has been Serious Professional Misconduct are those applied in deciding whether there has been negligence. That should be a prerequisite of a finding of Serious Professional Misconduct, but mere negligence should not be enough. Unfortunately, mere negligence has sometimes been enough: the Committee has sometimes taken its forensic cue more from the leader columns of outraged newspapers than from the columns of *Sidaway*.

## Capacity to consent
### General

Whether or not a particular patient has the capacity to consent is a question of fact in each case. If the patient can understand the nature of the relevant treatment, he generally has the capacity to consent validly to it. Thus most adult patients can give, or validly refuse to give, their consent to treatment.

Capacity is not an all or nothing thing. It can fluctuate, and one can have legal capacity for some purposes and not for others. A patient may be able to consent validly to the cutting of his toenails, but not to a triple heart bypass.

Assessment of capacity is essentially a medical business. The courts rarely get involved. When they do, they depend heavily on evidence from medical professionals.

### The test in Re C

In *Re C (Adult Refusal of Treatment)*[22] the court said that a patient

---

22. [1994] 1 WLR 290.

has the necessary capacity if he has the ability to:

(a) receive and retain information; and
(b) believe the information; and
(c) weigh the information, balancing the risks against the benefits.

It noted that a compulsive disorder or phobia may stifle belief in the information presented, annihilating capacity.

In *Re MB (an adult: medical treatment)*,[23] the Court of Appeal endorsed *Re C*, adding that "temporary factors" such as confusion, shock, pain, fatigue or drugs may completely erode capacity. It urged caution in concluding that one or more of these factors made a patient incapable. In relation to panic induced by fear, it said that *"... careful scrutiny of the evidence is necessary because fear of an operation may be a rational reason for refusal to undergo it. Fear may also, however, paralyse the will and thus destroy the capacity to make a decision."*

Having the capacity to consent does not mean that an objectively sensible decision will be made. As noted above, one cannot conclude that a patient does not have the necessary capacity because his decision endangers him. The cases urge judges to beware of assuming that somebody lacks capacity because he does not share the same values as the judge. A good illustration of this was the case of Miss B, which is discussed above.

That said, though, the judges are very ready to find incapacity in order to compel medical treatment, particularly where failure to have the treatment will endanger a third party. In some circumstances it is surprisingly easy to be mad. The courts are very ready to find that patients are suffering from mental disability. The

---

23. [1997] 2 FCR 541.

classic example is in *Re L (Patient: Non-consensual Treatment)*[24], which concerned a fear of needles.

## Capacity to consent
### Children

*What is a child?*
A child for these purposes is anyone under the age of 18. As will be seen, particular rules apply to 16 and 17 year olds.

*General principles: Consent to treatment is different from refusal of consent*
The law assumes that doctors who want to do things to children want to do them for good reasons. It therefore makes it more difficult validly to refuse treatment than to consent to treatment.

Consent to treatment can be obtained from a *Gillick*[25] competent child of any age, or a 16 or 17 year-old, or from a person with parental responsibility, or from the court.

So far as refusal of treatment is concerned, the consent of a person with parental responsibility trumps the refusal of a child of any age, and the consent of the court trumps the refusal of either.

In determining whether to exercise its power to override, the court will be ruled by the best interests test. The effect on the child's wider, non-medical interests of forcing treatment against the parents' wishes will of course be a relevant consideration, but is unlikely to be decisive against treatment. If parental co-operation with the treatment is vital to the treatment's success, the court may decline to order the treatment to go ahead, notwithstanding its view that the treatment, given proper compliance, would be in the

---

24. [1997] 8 Med LR 217.
25. *Gillick* competency is discussed below.

child's best interests, but such examples will be few and far between.[26] There will usually be ways (including, if it comes to that, wardship) of ensuring that the child can benefit from what the clinicians think it needs.

*General principles: Gillick competency*
The expression comes from *Gillick v. West Norfolk & Wisbech AHA*.[27] The idea is a simple and wholly common sensical one: a child should have capacity when in fact he can be demonstrated to have capacity. Legal presumptions should have no place in the determination of capacity. It should not be presumed that a child magically receives full capacity for all purposes at the age of 16 or 18, having been entirely incompetent beforehand.

The *Gillick* litigation concerned the obligation of doctors to consult with the parents of legal minors before giving contraceptive advice or prescriptions. The claimant, Victoria Gillick, said that it was outrageous that doctors could dispense with the parents' input. Not so, said the House of Lords, holding that as a matter of law a minor has the capacity to consent to medical treatment:

> *"... when the child achieves a sufficient understanding and intelligence to enable him or her to understand fully what is proposed."*[28]

Whether the child has that understanding and intelligence is a question of fact in each case.

Ability to understand fully what is proposed involves ability to

---

26. One example was *Re T (a minor) (wardship: medical treatment)* [1997] 1 WLR 242.
27. [1985] 3 All ER 402.
28. Per Lord Scarman at p. 423.

understand the consequences of a failure to treat - in other words to understand the risks-benefits equation which a competent medical practitioner will spell out.[29]

### Children between the ages of 16 and 18

As noted above, there is an important distinction between consent to treatment and refusal of consent to treatment. In relation to consent to treatment, the position is governed by statute:

Section 8 of the Family Law Reform Act 1969 provides that:

> *(1) The consent of a minor who has attained the age of 16 years to any surgical, medical or dental treatment which, in the absence of consent, would constitute a trespass to his person, shall be as effective as it would be if he were of full age; and where a minor has by virtue of this section given an effective consent to any treatment it shall not be necessary to obtain any consent for it from his parent or guardian.*
>
> *(2) In this section "surgical, medical or dental treatment" includes any procedure undertaken for the purposes of diagnosis, and this section applies to any procedure (including, in particular, the administration of an anaesthetic) which is ancillary to any treatment as it applies to that treatment.*
>
> *(3) Nothing in this section shall be construed as making ineffective any consent which would have been effective if this section had not been enacted."*

*W (A Minor) (Medical Treatment: Court's Jurisdiction)*[30]

---

29. Per Lord Donaldson MR in *Re R (a Minor) (wardship: medical treatment)* [1991] 4 All ER 177, 187.
30. [1992] 3 Med LR 317.

confirmed that this section does not apply to refusals of treatment. Where there is a refusal of treatment, anyone with parental responsibility, or the court, can impose treatment, assuming that the treatment is in the child's best interests.

*Children under the age of 16*
*Gillick* competent children can consent validly to treatment. Their refusal to consent can be trumped by a holder of parental responsibility or the court.

*Children who are already wards of court*
Even if the child seems capable of giving valid consent, the court's consent ought to be obtained anyway. This is more a rule of prudence and courtesy than of law.

**Patients with mental disorder**

There is a lot of confusion about this. It is certainly not the law that patients detained under the Mental Health Act 1983 can have anything done to them if the treating clinicians think it is in their best interests to do it. The 1983 Act does contain various provisions relating to consent to treatment for patients who are liable to be detained under those sections.[31] But those sections only authorise treatment in the absence of consent for the condition which brings the patient under the provisions of the Act in the first place.

For treatment which does not fall within these provisions, the normal law of consent applies. Some patients with mental disorder will be fully able to give or withhold consent. Remember that capacity is not an all or nothing thing; patients may have capacity

---

31. See ss.56-64.

for some things, and not for others. Where a patient with mental disorder does not have the capacity to consent to the proposed treatment, the usual rules apply; treatment will be lawful if it is in the patient's best interests.

## How are "best interests" determined?

The starting point is *F v. West Berkshire HA*.[32] This related to the sterilisation of a 36 year-old woman who suffered from serious mental disability. Lord Brandon concluded that an operation or other treatment performed on adult patients who are incapable of consenting would be lawful provided that it is in the best interests of the patients. It will be in their best interests:

> "... if, but only if, it is carried out in order either to save their lives or to ensure improvement or prevent deterioration in their physical or mental health."[33]

This is very wide indeed. The only treatment which falls outside this definition would seem to be treatment carried out experimentally or to gratify some sadistic impulse in the clinician concerned.

Controversially, the *Bolam* test was applied to the issue of how the patient's best interests should be determined. It is not difficult to imagine what the rhetoric of the civil liberties lobby said about that.

*F v. West Berkshire HA* is high authority. It cannot be dismissed. It was, however, quietly ignored. It has been replaced as a practitioner's guide by *Re SL (adult patient) (medical*

---

32. [1989] 2 All ER 545.
33. At p.551.

*treatment)*,³⁴ a fancy bit of forensic footwork by the Court of Appeal. Reliance on *Bolam* in *F* had the effect of ousting the supervisory jurisdiction of the court. *Re SL* reinstates it. It deploys a two stage test for deciding whether the proposed treatment is in the patient's best interests. First, would the treatment be endorsed by a responsible body of medical opinion? If no, the matter ends there. If yes, the second question is asked: Is the treatment *in fact* in this patient's best interests in these circumstances?

It is not just the court, on an application for a declaration, which must ask these questions. Doctors considering treatment without the patient's consent must ask them too. This has the logical effect of imposing a two stage duty on these doctors: to be *Bolam* reasonable and to act in the patient's best interests. The Court of Appeal has recently said that this is precisely the position.³⁵ What is logical for the court, though, can be artificial in practice, and this is surely an example. Would a responsible body of medical opinion really act contrary to the objective best interests of a patient?

It is well established that "best interests" means more than "best medical interests".³⁶ Evaluation of best interests is a holistic exercise. Thorpe LJ said, in *Re SL*:

> *"In deciding what is best for the disabled patient the judge must have regard to the patient's welfare as the paramount consideration. That embraces issues far wider than the medical. Indeed it would be undesirable and probably impossible to set bounds to what is relevant to a welfare*

---

34. [2000] 1 FCR 361.
35. See *Re A (medical treatment: male sterilisation)* [2000] 1 FCR 193.
36. See the famous *dictum* of Butler-Sloss LJ in *Re MB (an adult: medical treatment)* [1997] 8 Med LR 217 at 225: "Best interests are not limited to best medical interests."

*determination."*

This poses difficulties for doctors. They are obliged to act in a patient's best interests, but are told effectively that they will be in breach of their duty as doctors if they take merely medical criteria into account in deciding where the best interests lie. This wider enquiry into "best interests" may well be one which doctors simply do not have the time or the raw factual material to undertake. Any doctor in doubt about best interests in a non-emergency case is best advised to let the court, which has created all these problems, solve them.

**The doctrine of necessity**

In an emergency, where a patient is for some reason unable to consent, it is usually lawful to give the patient the treatment he needs.

There have been various legal analyses of this situation. The most commonly encountered in English law are (a) implied consent and (b) necessity.

Whatever the analysis adopted, there are limits to the treatment which can be legally carried out.

First, if it is known that in fact the patient would not consent for whatever reason to the treatment, it is illegal to do it. The classic cautionary tale is *Malette v. Shulman*.[37]

Second, the treating doctor should do no more than is reasonably required in the interests of the patient before he is again in a position to give valid consent.[38] This sounds straightforward, but is not. Suppose a patient is admitted unconscious to the

---

37. *Supra.*
38. See Lord Goff in *F v. West Berkshire HA, supra,* at p. 566.

casualty department. He has multiple compound fractures to his limbs. It is obvious that these will need internal fixation. The life threatening emergency, however, is bleeding from a divided femoral artery. Of course he cannot give consent to anything. The clinicians, invoking the doctrine of necessity, take him immediately to theatre to tie off the artery. It would clearly be in his best interests to do the internal fixation there and then. It would, however, be possible to wake him up, counsel him about the inevitable further surgery, get his consent to it, reanaesthetise him and get on with the surgery. A simple interpretation of this second caveat suggests that this is precisely what should be done. But since this result is clearly absurd, the courts would bend over backwards to avoid it. They would probably use the notion of implied consent to avoid it, saying that one impliedly consented to all inevitably necessary, although not immediately life-saving or consciousness-restoring procedures which it was sensible to provide at the same time as the life-saving or consciousness-restoring procedures.

Where an adult patient is incapable of consenting, it is common (and good) practice to consult the relatives about what to do. But their comments have no legal effect except insofar as they may evidence the attitude which the patient would have had towards the giving of consent for the relevant treatment.

The law does not require that consent is given in any particular way. Written consent forms, for instance, merely evidence valid consent; they do not constitute it.

**How can consent be given?**

There are no formal requirements. There is certainly no magic in consent forms.[39] They are just evidence. Often the very fact that the patient is in hospital for the planned procedure indicates that he has consented to the procedure (what else does he think he is there for?). But pieces of paper are reassuring for the lawyers.

**When to go to court**

Books on the law of consent are often written as if the court should determine capacity and the validity of consent in every case. Of course this is not so. The huge majority of dilemmas in the law of consent are resolved by clinicians, and resolved in a way that the Family Division would be very happy with. But nonetheless there are sometimes difficulties. The House of Lords has said that all cases of withdrawal of nutrition and hydration from patients in PVS should go before the court.[40] It is conventional, and wise, to take several other classes of case there too. The best example is the proposed sterilisation of patients.[41] Despite the Court of Appeal deploring applications in several other types of case unless there is real doubt about capacity,[42] the mood of the Family Division is to encourage recourse to the court. Where there is uncertainty about capacity which cannot be resolved satisfactorily with the clinicians, or where there is dispute with relatives, clinicians are well advised to get the court to endorse any proposed action.

---

39. In *Chatterton v. Gerson, supra,* at 265, Bristow J said: *"Getting the patient to sign a pro forma expressing consent to undergo the operation 'the effect and nature of which have been explained to me' ... should be a valuable reminder to ... everyone of the need for explanation and consent. But it would be no defence to an action based on trespass to the person if no explanation had in fact been given. The consent would have been expressed in form only, not in reality."*
40. *Airedale NHS Trust v. Bland, supra.*
41. See *Re S (Sterilisation)* [2000] 2 FLR 389: cp *Re GF* [1992] 1 FLR 293.
42. See, for instance, *St. George's Healthcare NHS Trust v. S* [1999] Fam. 36.

## The potential impact of the Human Rights Act 1998 on the Law of Consent
### General

This Act came into force in October 2000. It grafts the European Convention on Human Rights into English law.

Nobody knows how it will affect the law of consent. But various people have speculated. Some of those speculations follow.

So far as the influence of the Human Rights Act is concerned, two categories of case have to be distinguished. These are *Sidaway*-type cases, in which consent is inadequate because the information necessary for proper consent to be given has not been disclosed, and other consent to treatment cases.

Broadly, *Sidaway*-type cases could well be affected by the Act: other consent to treatment cases are unlikely to be.

## Consent to treatment
### Non-Sidaway type cases and the Human Rights Act
*Article 8 considerations*

Any treatment without consent, however minor, engages Article 8(1), which provides:

> "*Everyone has the right to respect for his private and family life, his home and his correspondence.*"

But that is not the end of the matter. By Article 8(2), an infringement of this right may be justified if it is:

> "*... in accordance with the law and is necessary in a democratic society in the interests of national security, public safety or the economic well-being of the country, for the prevention of disorder or crime, for the protection of health or morals, or for the protection of the rights and freedoms of

*others."*

"... in accordance with the law" means permitted by domestic law. The Commission has said that it will intervene in questions of national law if it is "arbitrary or unreasonable",[43] but it is inconceivable that the ECHR would take that attitude towards the English law of consent, which is relatively enlightened.

"... necessary in a democratic society" is a strange, vague phrase. The Commission apparently thinks that in compulsory treatment cases it invokes a simple question: do the advantages of treatment outweigh the disadvantages?[44] However critical one is of the paternalism of *F v. West Berkshire HA*, the English law is more demanding and more stoutly protective of Article 8(1) right than this.

Compulsory treatment cases have relied on many of the cited interests under Article 8(2) to justify interference with the basic Article 8(1) right. Examples include public safety (for vaccination and screening programmes[45]), the prevention of disorder or crime (for compulsory blood tests for drunk drivers[46] and drug tests for prisoners[47]), and the protection of the rights and freedoms of others (for compulsory blood tests in a paternity suit[48]). In every case the approach of the court or the Commission indicates that English consent law, from an Article 8 perspective, is whiter than white. Analyses of the law of consent in terms of the Convention add little to the old common law analyses. A classic example is the recent case of Leslie Burke, which is considered in detail in

---

43. *Peters v. Netherlands* (1994) 77-A DR 75 at 79.
44. *Acmanne v. Belgium* (1985) 40 DR 251.
45. *Acmanne, supra.*
46. *X v. Netherlands* (1978) App. No. 8239/78.
47. *Peters v. Netherlands* (1994) 77-A DR 75.
48. *X v. Austria* (1979) 18 DR 154.

Chapter 5.[49]

The court's trumping of parental decisions about children's treatment is one area where one might expect Article 8 to be vocal. In practice the courts have said that the English law's overriding concern for the welfare of the child satisfies Article 8, just as it satisfies the UN Convention on the Rights of the Child.[50]

*Article 3 considerations*
Article 3 provides, baldly, that

"*No one shall be subjected to torture or to inhuman or degrading treatment or punishment.*"

There are none of the qualifying caveats of Article 8.

Article 3 seems a very long way from medicine. But the European Court's legal geography is not everybody's.

In a lot of anxious consideration in Strasbourg, "degrading" has been held to have its natural meaning.[51]

Generally, of course, bona fide medical treatment, even given without valid consent, is unlikely to be degrading. This was acknowledged in *Herczegfalvy v. Austria*,[52] where it was held that:

"*as a general rule, a measure which is a therapeutic necessity cannot be regarded as inhuman or degrading.*"

---

49. See *R. v. General Medical Council, ex parte Burke* [2004] EWHC 1879.
50. Article 3(1) of the Convention says: "*In all actions concerning children, whether undertaken by public or private social welfare institutions, courts of law, administrative authorities or legislative bodies, the best interests of the child shall be a primary consideration.*" See too *Garcia v. Switzerland*, Application No. 10148/82.
51. *Ireland v. UK* (1978) 2 EHRR 25 at para. 167: *East African Asians Cases* (1973) 3 EHRR 76 at 80.
52. (1993) 15 EHRR 437 at para.82.

This begs two questions:

(a) what constitutes therapeutic necessity? and,
(b) when does the general rule not apply?

What is meant by "therapeutic necessity" is far from clear. The opinion in *Herczegfalvy* refers[53] to treatment which is *"necessary from the medical point of view and carried out in conformity with standards accepted by medical science,"* but then[54] to treatment which *"could reasonably be considered to be justified by medical considerations,"* apparently a much lower standard.

Usually quibbles like this will be unnecessary. Whatever is meant, treatment outside Dr. Mengele's surgery, even without consent, is unlikely to be therapeutically unnecessary. And if it is, doing it will be actionable in the domestic law of negligence and/or assault. So the Article adds nothing. Certainly the domestic law cannot be said to fall short of the protection offered by Article 3.

It is also wholly unclear when the general rule will not apply. From the opinion (rather than the judgment of the Court) the type of departure from the general rule that seems to be envisaged in *Herczegfalvy* is where the force used to administer otherwise necessary treatment renders the whole process inhuman or degrading. It is not clear from *Herczegfalvy*, though, whether it matters whether the patient is capable of consenting or not. *Herczegfalvy* was a hunger strike case. The "treatment" concerned was force feeding. There were doubts there about the patient's capacity. One would have thought on first principles that one did not need much capacity to make a decision as basic as that. He certainly seemed capable of indicating pretty decisively that he did not want to be fed, as the ribs broken and teeth lost in his struggles

---

53. At p. 468.
54. At p. 469.

with the feeders showed. There was muted disapproval of the amount of force used, but it was held that there had been no breach of Article 3.[55] It is a rather undemanding Article.

So far things are unclear enough. But it gets worse. The already impenetrably murky waters of Article 3 have been further muddied by *X v Denmark*.[56] There it was held that medical treatment, even with consent, could be a breach of Article 3 if it was "experimental". *X* is a highly unsatisfactory case which raises more questions than it answers. "Experimental" was undefined. In *X* itself new, and fairly untested, equipment was used to carry out the operation consented to. In fact it carried a greater risk to the patient than the conventional equipment. This, however, was not considered to be "experimental". It was further held that experimental treatment would only constitute a breach "under certain circumstances," but it was not indicated what those circumstances might be.

What all this comes to is that while it is possible for examiners to devise improbably exotic scenarios in hospitals which should inspire the better candidates to write about Article 3, it is unlikely to add much to the way in which consent cases are fought in practice in English law. In each of the Strasbourg cases cited, domestic English law is more demanding than Article 3.

One might have thought, however, that Article 3 might genuinely have had something new to say about the treatment of unconscious patients. But as the English law presently stands, it is not clear that it does. One line of authority suggests that in order to be protected by the Article one has to be able to appreciate the

---

55. Interestingly, it was also held that there had been no breach of Article 8, on the grounds that he did not have the capacity to consent. However, the consideration of Article 8 can be politely described as skimpy.
56. (1983) 32 DR 282.

inhuman or degrading treatment.[57] This issue is considered in detail in Chapter 5.

## Consent to treatment
### *Sidaway-type cases and the Human Rights Act*

The real threat to *Sidaway* is not via a threat to *Bolam*, on which *Sidaway* is parasitic,[58] but by an independent challenge under Article 3 and/or Article 8. The possible effects of these Articles to issues of consent to treatment generally are discussed below.

On its face, Article 8 does not look like a principle which has anything much medical about it. But it metastasises dangerously throughout the whole corpus of law.

In *X v. UK*[59] it was held that Article 8 could be breached where there was a failure to inform a patient properly about a medical procedure.[60] Little has been heard of *X v. UK* since. It seemed to say that there would have to be a fairly gross failure for a breach to be established.

But recently the language of Article 8 has been stretched painfully. Thus, for instance, in *Guerra and others v. Italy*[61] Article 8 has been held to require authorities to provide individuals with information relevant to the safety of their homes and their physical and mental well-being. In *Guerra*[62] there was a failure to provide residents of a village with information about a dangerous factory nearby. It was held that the villagers' right to private and family

---

57. *NHS Trust A v. M* [2001] 2 WLR 942; cp *R. v. General Medical Council, ex parte Burke* [2004] EWHC 1879.
58. The ECHR threat to *Bolam* is discussed in detail in Chapter 4.
59. (1978) 14 DR 31.
60. But in the context of that case (vaccination) there was in fact no breach, since all parents knew that vaccinations carried some risk.
61. (1998) 26 EHRR 357.
62. In which *X v. UK* was not cited.

life included a right to:

> "... essential information that would have enabled them to assess the risks they and their families might run if they continued to live [there] ..."

If it can stretch that far, it might well extend to imposing an obligation of full disclosure of all conceivably relevant facts when taking consent from patients.[63] And it could well have some impact on the compulsory treatment of persons under a disability.

The extension of the *Bolam* test to the law of consent (in *Sidaway*) has always been controversial, and the House of Lords in *Sidaway* itself was not unanimous about it. The courts are likely to say that issues of consent should be resolved not by asking whether a responsible body of medical opinion would have divulged something, but whether an absolute right to information conferred by Article 8 has been infringed. The considerations which are likely to make *Bolam* invulnerable to an Article 2 challenge are unlikely to be found to make *Sidaway* invulnerable to Article 8.

---

63. The courts would be likely to apply a "reasonable patient" type test. *Bolam* may not survive in this context.

# CHAPTER 3

# CONFIDENTIALITY

## Introduction

Clinical secrets matter. The law is concerned about them for two main reasons. First the pragmatic reason. If there were no law protecting medical confidences, clinicians would gossip about their patients. That would be against the interests of the doctors and the patients. The patients would feel inhibited in disclosing important information. The doctors would be deprived of important details, and get things wrong. The other reason is more philosophical. The judges think that human autonomy is important, and that autonomy is violated if people talk about you in an unauthorised way.

There are lots of ways in which the law has described breaches of confidence. Those ways cannot and need not be reconciled. It really does not matter whether one thinks of a breach of confidence as a breach of trust, or a tort, or something in between. Sometimes it helps to think of confidences like personal property; sometimes that analysis produces ridiculous results. Almost every lay person can work out the legally correct result in breach of confidence cases. The language used by the courts to justify their own conclusions about such cases is so various that almost every lay person could produce a judgment in most confidence cases which would get past the Court of Appeal.

In this chapter, to avoid controversy, I will talk bet-hedgingly about the "quasi-tort of breach of confidence."

Although the common law of breach of confidence is still very important, statute has interfered. Statute has, however, done little more than codify the common law. Understand the common law and you know the statutes intuitively.

## The elements of the quasi-tort of breach of confidence

For a breach of confidence to be actionable (which means for it to entitle a claimant to damages or some other remedy), the claimant has to prove:

(a) disclosure of information in circumstances of confidence; and
(b) unauthorised disclosure of the information; and
(c) that the public interest in non-disclosure outweighs the public interest in disclosure. This may be decided according to a test of good conscience (see below); and
(d) that the information disclosed is not already in the public domain.

Each of these elements is considered in turn.

### *Disclosure of information in circumstances of confidence*

Forget this, in medical contexts. Or rather assume it. There is lots of law which deals with what amounts to "circumstances of confidence". It is all a matter of feel. All conceivable exchanges of medical information take place in circumstances which the law regards as confidential.

### *Unauthorised disclosure of the information*

This is more tricky. At this point the law of confidentiality imports the law of consent. A doctor can with impunity sell a patient's most intimate medical secrets to the tabloids if the patient consents. On the other hand the doctor is in grave jeopardy if he mentions a highly clinically relevant and not at all embarrassing fact to the treating consultant if the patient insists that that consultant must not be told.

It is rare for a patient to state expressly that his confidences must be respected. Patients assume that doctors will honour confidences, but also assume that the clinical information will be disseminated to those people (and only those people) who need, for clinical purposes, to know. They, therefore, impliedly consent to that dissemination. The obvious question is: who needs to know? It is arguably not necessary, for instance, for the nurses to know all the clinical details; their remit is a narrow one. Yet medical and nursing notes are increasingly integrated, and nurses will often discover, as they consult the notes for their own purposes, confidential details which do not bear on their own job. In those circumstances has there been an actionable breach of confidence? And what about the white boards behind the nurses' station which confront every visitor to every hospital ward? They have the patients' names on them, and often other clinical information of a highly sensitive kind, such as an instruction that the patient should be barrier nursed (indicating a reduced immune status or an infectious disease). Is the broadcast of these details unlawful?

Questions like this have not been tested in the English courts. It is suggested that the courts would find that, absent an explicit prohibition on disclosure to particular people, a patient impliedly consents not only to that disclosure which is strictly clinically necessary, but also to that disclosure which is incidental to the practice of medicine. Put another way, he impliedly consents to that disclosure which it is not reasonably practicable to avoid.

Hospitals should not rest too heavily on this principle. The white board example comes close to the mark. There is an obvious benefit to the running of hospitals in having the white board information readily available without the need to rummage through notes, but is it not reasonably practicable to devise an alternative to the promiscuous publication of this information which the boards entail?

## The public interest in non-disclosure outweighs the public interest in disclosure

If there has been unauthorised disclosure of confidential information, the disclosure will be actionable in the courts (subject to the caveat about information already in the public domain) if the public interest in its disclosure is not outweighed by the public interest in its non-disclosure. The word "public" here is important. It used to be thought that the individual whose confidence was being breached had a private interest which was in competition against the public interest. It is now clear that even if rights of confidence can for some purposes be analysed as private interests analogous to property rights (as in some cases they can), when it comes to the weighing of interests, public is weighed against public.

How the courts conduct this balancing exercise is illustrated by two classic cases:

*(a) Disclosure is justified: W v. Egdell*[1]
W was a paranoid schizophrenic with a number of killings and maimings to his credit. He was duly detained in a secure hospital. Twelve years after the start of his detention he applied to a mental health review tribunal. To support his application he obtained a report from Dr. Egdell, a consultant psychiatrist. The report did not say what W hoped. Instead it said that he was desperately dangerous, and that his continued interest in home-made bombs was incompatible with a safe and useful life in the community. W disappointedly withdrew his application to the tribunal. He refused to consent to the disclosure of Dr. Egdell's report to the hospital medical officer. Dr. Egdell was unhappy about this non-disclosure.

---

1. [1990] 1 Ch 359.

He thought that if it was not known that W was still dangerous, others might be endangered. He therefore disclosed the report to the hospital medical officer. Copies eventually reached the Secretary of State and the DHSS.

W found out about the disclosure and was furious. He issued proceedings for breach of confidence. There was an obvious, unauthorised breach of confidence. The only question was whether the breach was actionable. The case reached the Court of Appeal. The court dismissed W's claim, saying:

(i) There is a public interest in a doctor keeping his patients' confidences.

(ii) This public interest is not the only public interest in play; there is a competing public interest in protecting others from crime.

(iii) The nature of W's crimes meant that it was in the public interest that those responsible for him knew the truth about his criminal thoughts and aspirations. Dr. Egdell's report was clearly relevant to those managing W.

(iv) The disclosure was proper, whether one looked at the propriety simply in terms of competing public interests or in terms of the General Medical Council's guidelines on confidentiality.

(v) Only the most compelling circumstances would justify a breach of medical confidence. These circumstances were compelling.

(vi) Article 8(1) of the ECHR may protect an individual against the disclosure of information which is transmitted in circumstances of professional confidence. But Article 8(1) had to be read together with 8(2), which envisaged that there may be circumstances in which a public authority might legitimately interfere with the exercise of an Article 8(1) right in accordance with the law and where necessary in the interests of public safety or the prevention of crime. If and insofar as there was any interference with W's Article 8(1) right by a public authority, that interference fell squarely within the Article 8(2) exception, and accordingly there was no breach of Article 8.

### (b) Disclosure is not justified: X v Y and others[2]

Employees of the claimant health authority told the first defendant, a newspaper reporter, that two general practitioners continued to practise despite having AIDS. The second defendant, a newspaper, paid for the information. The health authority obtained an order restraining the defendants from publishing or otherwise using the information. Nonetheless the newspaper published an article written by the defendant reporter headed "Scandal of Docs with AIDS". The gist was that there were doctors in England with AIDS who continued to practise, and that the DHSS knew all about it. The implication was that the DHSS wanted to suppress the information. The claimant went to court seeking, *inter alia*, an injunction restraining publication of the names of the GPs. There were predictable issues about contempt of court, but the interest of the case in this context is that the defendants argued that the public interest in the naming of the GPs outweighed the public interest in non-disclosure. The argument failed, Rose J saying:

> "*I keep in the forefront of my mind the very important public interest in freedom of the press. And I accept that there is some public interest in knowing that which defendants seek to publish ... But in my judgment those public interests are*

---

2. [1988] 2 All ER 648.

*substantially outweighed when measured against the public interests in relation to loyalty and confidentiality both generally and with particular reference to AIDS patients' hospital records. There has been no misconduct by the [claimants]. The records of hospital patients, particularly those suffering from this appalling condition should, in my judgment, be as confidential as the courts can properly keep them in order that the [claimants] my be 'free from suspicion that they are harbouring disloyal employees'. The [claimants] have 'suffered a grievous wrong in which the defendants became involved ... with active participation'. The deprivation of the public of the information sought to be published will be of minimal significance if the injunction is granted; for, without it, all the evidence before me shows that a wide-ranging public debate about AIDS generally and about its effect on doctors is taking place among doctors of widely differing views, within and without the BMA, in medical journals and in many newspapers, including the Observer, the Sunday Times and the Daily Express. Indeed, the sterility of the defendants' argument is demonstrated by the edition of the second defendant's own newspaper dated 22 March 1987. It is there expressly stated, purportedly quoting a Mr. Milligan, that three general practitioners two of whom are practising (impliedly in Britain) have AIDS. Paraphrasing Templeman LJ in the Schering case,³ the facts, in the most limited form now sought to be published, have already been made available and may again be made available if they are known otherwise than through the medium of the informer. The risk of identification is only one factor in assessing whether to permit the use of confidential information. In my judgment to allow*

---

3. *Schering Chemicals Ltd v. Falkman Ltd* [1981] 2 All ER 321.

> *publication in [a] ... restricted form would be to enable both defendants to procure breaches of confidence and then to make their own selection for publication. This would make a mockery of the law's protection of confidentiality when no justifying public interest has been shown. These are the considerations which guide me, whether my task is properly described as a balancing exercise, or an exercise in judicial judgment, or both ... "*[4]

*A public interest defence?*
Practitioners often talk about a "public interest defence" to an allegation of breach of confidence. It does not matter much, but the better view is that this is technically wrong. It is part of the definition of an actionable breach of confidence that disclosure is not justified in the public interest.

*Another way of looking at it: Professional conscience as the arbiter of liability*
The Court of Appeal in *Egdell* was evidently influenced by the fact that the GMC would have smiled on Dr. Egdell's disclosure. What was an influence in *Egdell* now seems to be a factor effectively determinative of liability.

In *R. v. Department of Health, ex parte Source Informatics Ltd*,[5] a case about the supply of information by pharmacists to data collection companies, Simon Brown LJ said, having reviewed the authorities:

> *"To my mind the one clear and consistent theme emerging from all these authorities is this: the confidant is placed under a duty of good faith to the confider and the touchstone by*

---

4. At 661.
5. [2000] Lloyd's Rep. Med. 76.

*which to judge the scope of his duty and whether or not it has been fulfilled or breached is his own conscience, no more and no less. One asks, therefore, on the facts of this case: would a reasonable pharmacist's conscience be troubled by the proposed use to be made of patients' prescriptions? Would he think that by entering [the data collection agency's] scheme he was breaking his customers' confidence, making unconscientious use of the information they provide? ... The concern of the law is to protect the confider's personal privacy. That and that alone is the right at issue in this case. The patient has no proprietorial claim to the prescription form or to the information it contains. Of course he can bestow or withhold his custom as he pleases – the pharmacist, note, has no such right: he is by law bound to dispense to whoever presents a prescription. But that gives the patient no property in the information and no right to control its use provided only and always that his privacy is not put at risk ... This appeal concerns, as all agree, the application of a broad principle of equity. I propose its resolution on a similarly broad basis ... I would stand back from the many detailed arguments addressed to us and hold simply that pharmacists' consciences ought not reasonably to be troubled by cooperation with [the data collection agency's] proposed scheme. The patient's privacy will have been safeguarded, not invaded. The pharmacist's duty of confidence will not have been breached."*[6]

This is a return to the old line of authority which regarded the quasi-tort of breach of confidence as a creature of equity. It welds law and ethics. Disclosure will be justified if a professional with a

---

6. 82-83.

rightly oriented conscience would disclose. A rightly oriented conscience is defined by reference to the disciplinary codes of the relevant profession. This is rather odd. It indicates that the courts are ready to regard the conscience of the ethically sound professional as the effective arbiter of the public interest balancing exercise – an abdication, really, of the court's own arbitral responsibility. The balancing exercise at least implies an element of objectivity: the conscience test is nakedly subjective. Probably the courts have adopted this test out of deference to the complexity of professional decision-making. They have acknowledged that the doctors know more about the agonised dilemmas of medical disclosure than the courts can. Effectively a sort of *Bolam* test has been imported into the adjudication of medical confidentiality cases. The standard required may be higher than *Bolam* would demand, but the principle is similar. A doctor will be excused for an unauthorised disclosure if a responsible body of doctors who live their lives by the GMC rule book would have disclosed in the same circumstances. The practical effect is that the GMC rules have become part of the substantive law of medical confidentiality, or, if one wants to conflate the conscience test and the public interest balancing test, compliance with the GMC guidelines indicates that the individual doctor has weighed appropriately the public interests in disclosure and non-disclosure, and acted accordingly.

## The information disclosed is not already in the public domain

The courts realise that there is no point in trying to close the stable door after the horse has bolted. The old equitable maxim applies: equity is not in vain. Equity will therefore not give a pointless remedy. If a patient's medical secrets appear on the front page of the national papers, not only will he not be able to get an injunction restraining further disclosure, but a doctor who has not read the papers but knows those secrets from a confidential consultation will not be committing an actionable breach of confidence if he gossips about the secrets in the hospital canteen.

## Statutory intervention
### General

Statutes and statutory instruments can:

(a) Make the disclosure of confidential information compulsory where that disclosure would otherwise be unlawful.
(b) Make the disclosure of confidential information permissible where that disclosure would otherwise be unlawful.
(c) Buttress the common law of confidentiality by codifying that law and providing penalties for unauthorised disclosure.

Category (a) can be considered separately. Categories (b) or (c) will be considered together.

## Statutory provisions about compulsory disclosure
### General

There are many examples. They include notification of abortions to the Chief Medical Officer,[7] notification of specified notifiable diseases to the local authority,[8] and notification of births to the

---

7. Abortion Regulations 1991: SI 1991/499.
8. Public Health (Control of Disease) Act 1984; Public Health (Infectious Diseases) Regulations 1988: SI 1988/1546.

district medical officer.[9]

## Road Traffic Act 1988

One of the more controversial examples is section 170(b) of the Road Traffic Act 1988. This provides that where the driver of a vehicle or the rider of a bicycle is alleged to be guilty of a road traffic offence *"any other person shall if required ... give such information which it is in his power to give and may lead to the identification of the driver."* That such information may have been obtained in circumstances of professional confidentiality is no defence to a charge of failure to disclose when required under this section to do so. Some of the corollaries of this in relation to genetic information are considered in Chapter 1.

## Prevention of Terrorism

Under the Prevention of Terrorism (Temporary Provisions) Act 1989,[10] it is an offence for anyone with certain information about terrorists to refuse to disclose it. Again, there are no exceptions for information disclosed in the course of medical consultations.

## Police seizure of medical records

Another form of compulsory disclosure is a requirement to hand over medical records. The police have various powers to enter premises and seize confidential medical records. Most medical records will be "excluded material" within the meaning of the Police and Criminal Evidence Act 1984, and so can only be seized

---

9. National Health Service Act 1977, s.124(4); National Health Service (Notification of Births and Deaths) Regulations 1982: SI 1982/286.
10. This has been renewed annually since 1989.

after an application to a circuit judge.[11]

**Defence requests for medical records**

Sometimes defence solicitors in criminal cases will ask for medical records – typically of a victim of an alleged offence who witholds consent to disclosure. The only safe advice to doctors in this situation is to sit tight, refuse disclosure, wait for a witness summons and wait for the court to rule on whether or not there should be disclosure.[12]

**Disclosure for civil proceedings: The general rule and public interest immunity**

There is a mass of complex law about what must be disclosed where civil litigation is contemplated or pending. Detailed consideration is outside the scope of this book.[13] Broadly, all documents relevant to the issues in civil litigation which are in the control of the parties must be disclosed, provided that the extent of and effort involved in the disclosure is in proportion to the seriousness and value of the litigation. Generally, if somebody chooses to litigate, he chooses to waive the rights to confidentiality

---

11. "Excluded material" includes personal records acquired or created in the course of a trade, business, profession or other occupation or for the purposes of any paid or unpaid office which are held in confidence: see s.11(1)(a). Personal records include any documentary any other records relating to a person's physical or mental health: see s.12(a). However, if the police do not have the appropriate warrant, but are on the premises for another purpose and have reasonable grounds for believing that the material is evidence relevant for their investigation and needs to be seized to prevent it being destroyed, they may seize it: see s.19.
12. The witness summons will be issued under the Criminal Procedure (Attendance of Witnesses) Act 1965, as amended by the Criminal Procedure and Investigations Act 1996.
13. It is considered in detail in the context of medical confidentiality in Clinical Confidentiality, Foster C and Peacock N, Monitor Press, 2000.

in documents which are relevant to that litigation. Documents can be obtained from non-parties to civil litigation, and non-party doctors are again often asked to disclose the records of non-parties to the litigation. Again, the sit-tight rule applies: a doctor asked for the records of a non-party to litigation should say no, and wait for the witness summons.

The general rule that relevant documents should be disclosed, provided that disclosure is proportionate, is subject to an important caveat: public interest immunity. This is where someone holding documents which are relevant says: "I will not disclose these documents. The public interest in preserving the confidentiality of the document outweighs the public interest in securing justice."[14]

Public interest immunity can be divided into two categories: class immunity (where all documents which fall into a particular class are immune from disclosure), and non-class immunity (where immunity from disclosure will depend on the contents of the particular document in question).

Documents which attract class immunity include, predictably and classically, documents relating to national security. It is doubtful whether any of the classes of documents routinely in issue in medical litigation fall into any immune class.[15]

Individual document public interest immunity does have a real part to play in medical litigation, however. The public interest which has been identified in many of the cases is the public interest in ensuring the free flow of information between patient and

---

14. Based on the classic formulation of Lord Templeman in *R. v. Chief Constable of West Midlands, ex parte Wiley* [1994] 3 WLR 433 at 436. Where public interest immunity is invoked to prevent the disclosure of documents which would otherwise be used for litigation, the test is not the balance of public interests in disclosure and non-disclosure, but whether in the absence of disclosure a fair trial is possible: see *R. v. H* [2004] 2 AC 134.
15. See *Mercer v. St. Helens and Knowsley Hospitals NHS Trust* (1995) CLY 95/4124; *Copp v. Chief Constable of Avon and Somerset Police* (1997) CLY 97/463.

doctor. It is recognised that indiscriminate disclosure will inhibit that flow. This was the policy which lay behind the decision in *R. v. K*.[16] A defendant in a criminal trial sought disclosure of the video of an interview which had been made at a children's hospital for therapeutic purposes. The hospital refused disclosure, asserting public interest immunity. The Court of Appeal, while criticising the trial judge for refusing to see the video before adjudicating on disclosure, agreed with the hospital's contentions.[17] It must be strongly arguable that public interest immunity attaches, on similar grounds, to documentation produced in the course of hospital audit, particularly where the results of the audit depend heavily on confidential comments by clinicians about themselves and their colleagues.

## Rights of access to health records

Patients' rights of access to their health records are examples, too, of compulsory disclosure.

The general rule, absent statute but buttressed by the Patients' Charter[18] and NHS circulars,[19] is that patients should have access to their own records if it is in their best interests to do so. Of course it will not always be in their best interests. Medical records can have some very disturbing things in them. There is no common law right of access, or any right under ECHR Article 8 to medical records if the holder of the records reasonably concludes that it is not in the patient's best interests to see them.[20]

---

16. (1993) 97 Cr App Rep 342.
17. See also *Ellis v. Home Office* [1953] 2 QB 135; *R. v. Secretary of State for the Home Office, ex parte Benson*, unreported, 1 November 1988; *Williams v. Star Newspaper Co Ltd* (1908) 24 LTR 297.
18. Published by the Department of Health, 1996.
19. Eg, Health Service Guidance (91)(6).
20. See *R. v. Mid Glamorgan FHSA, ex parte Martin* [1995] 1 WLR 110.

The Data Protection Act 1998 gives "data subjects" a general right of access to their personal data.[21] But this general right is subject to an important caveat which parallels the common law right to withhold damaging information. If access is likely to cause serious harm to the physical or mental health of the data subject, access can lawfully be denied.[22] Access cannot be denied simply on the ground that a third party is identified in the records unless serious harm is likely to be caused to that third party by disclosure.[23] The 1998 Act gives no right of access by third parties.

The Access to Medical Reports Act 1988 gives patients the right to see certain medical reports compiled about them for the purposes of employment or insurance. Access can be denied if disclosure would be likely to cause serious harm to the individual or to others; or would (in the obscure and sinister words of the Act) "indicate the intentions of the practitioner in respect of the individual" or would reveal the identity of a third party (other than a health professional involved in the individual's care) who has not consented to being named.[24]

The Access to Health Records Act 1990 used to be very important. It has now been rendered almost wholly obsolete by the Data Protection Act 1998, but limps on, dealing with access to the records of dead people.

**Other statutory provisions regulating and codifying disclosure**

The big one here is the Data Protection Act 1998. It puts into place some rigorous safeguards for controlling and releasing data, which

---

21. Section 7.
22. See the Data Protection (Subject Access Modification) (Health) Order 2000: SI 2000/413, Article 5(1).
23. Article 8.
24. Section 7.

it enforces by criminal sanction.

It creates two categories of data of particular importance in medical law: "Personal data" (which can lead to the identification of a living individual)[25] and "sensitive personal data", which includes "information as to ... [the] physical or mental health and condition" of the data subject.[26]

Personal data and sensitive personal data can only be dealt with in any way ("processed" is the word the Act uses) if the processing is in accordance with the "data protection principles."

In a medical law context six of these principles are of paramount importance:

(a) The first principle: personal data may only be processed fairly and lawfully.
(b) The third principle: personal data shall be adequate, relevant and not excessive.
(c) The fourth principle: personal data shall be accurate and kept up to date.
(d) The fifth principle: personal data shall not be kept for any longer than necessary for the purpose for which they were processed.
(e) The seventh principle: adequate technical and organisational measures shall be taken to prevent unauthorised or unlawful processing of such data, and against loss, destruction or damage.
(f) The eighth principle: personal data may not be transferred outside the European Economic Area unless the recipient country or territory has adequate levels of protection for the rights and freedoms of data subjects.

---

25. Section 1(1).
26. Section 2(e).

These principles speak for themselves. In their application to most communication of and recording of data for medical purposes they reflect and in some cases magnify the common law of confidentiality. Detailed consideration of each of these elements is outside the scope of this book, and in any event would be mostly speculative, since there has as yet been relatively little litigation on the principles in medical contexts.

There has been a good deal of concern about s.60 of the Health and Social Care Act 2001. Section 60(1) provides that *"The Secretary of State may by regulations make such provision for and in connection with requiring or regulating the processing of prescribed patient information for medical purposes as he considers necessary or expedient (a) in the interests of improving patient care, or (b) in the public interest."*

No regulations have yet been made under this section. The section is intended to facilitate medical research and audit by allowing the disclosure (which would otherwise be legally dubious) of patient information. The watchdogs have their eyes pinned to this section.

## The Freedom of Information Act 2000

A piece of US inspired legislation is waiting in the wings. On 30 November 2005 the Freedom of Information Act 2000 will come fully into force. It sounds a lot more important than it is. Its main effect will be to create a massive and expensive bureaucracy for responding to requests for information. Only utterly innocuous information need be disclosed.

The details of its provisions are outside the scope of this book, but its general effect will be that if any person asks a public authority for information, he is entitled to be informed in writing whether or not that information is held, and if it is held, to be supplied with the information. The Act sets time limits for the authority's compliance.

There are, predictably, several categories of information which are exempt from disclosure under the Act. These include information which the applicant can get in another way, information which the authority intends to publish in the future, information supplied by the security services, or information which, if disclosed, might prejudice the defence, the international relations or the relations between domestic administrative bodies in the UK. This latter class is yawningly wide and could be used by a paranoid Minister to make the Act entirely irrelevant to all information held by national or local government. Information relating to the investigation of criminal proceedings is similarly exempt, as is information obtained or recorded for the purposes of civil proceedings brought by the authority where the information comes from confidential sources – clearly a provision of dizzying circularity: information is confidential if it is confidential. Information which might, if disclosed, prejudice law enforcement, is exempt, and so is information held by a public authority for the purpose of audit functions, the formulation of government policy, the effective conduct of public affairs (the author challenges anyone to find any information which could not be dressed up to look like that), health and safety, and so on.

Personal information is exempt, as is information provided in confidence.

This Act is unlikely to have any significant effect on disclosure in a medical context. Health records will remain exempt. The Act will not compel disclosure of otherwise unobtainable but significant NHS audit material, and ironically might be used to block the disclosure of material like that which at present is disclosed. There will no doubt be a lot of litigation about the extent to which the exemptions are compatible with Article 8 of the

ECHR. The answer will certainly be, in the huge majority of cases, that the statutory exemptions mirror precisely and lawfully the provisions of Article 8(2).

**The effect of the ECHR**

When the Human Rights Act 1998 became law in England, some thought that Article 8 of the ECHR would revolutionise the law of confidentiality. This has simply not happened.

Article 8 is headed: "Right to respect for private and family life, home and correspondence". Its text reads:

> "*1. Everyone has the right to respect for his private and family life, his home and his correspondence.*
>
> *2. There shall be no interference by a public authority with the exercise of this right except such as is in accordance with the law and is necessary in a democratic society in the interests of national security, public safety or the economic well-being of the country, for the prevention of disorder or crime, for the protection of health or morals, or for the protection of the rights and freedoms of others.*"

The attitude of the English courts has been that the common law of confidentiality (embodying as it does a balancing of interests exactly analogous to the balancing of Article 8(1) and Article 8(2) criteria) and the statutory provisions (most of which either contain similar "balancing" provisions or are straightforward examples of Article 8(2) exceptions) are compliant with Article 8.[27] The reported decisions of the Strasbourg Court and the Commission on

---

27. See, for example, *R. v. Mid Glamorgan Family Health Services, ex parte Martin, supra.*

Article 8 matters which touch on medicine are all decisions which the English courts, applying domestic law, could well have made.[28]

---

28. See, for example, *MS v. Sweden*, 23 EHRR 313; *Z v. Finland*, 25 EHRR 371; *Andersson (Anne-Marie) v. Sweden*, 25 EHRR 722.

CHAPTER 4

# CLINICAL NEGLIGENCE

## Introduction

This is big business. Many thousands of claims are brought, and a fair number (although a small proportion) succeed. Clinical negligence is the basic, gas-bill paying professional diet of most lawyers practising medical law. The principles are broadly the same as in most personal injury actions, but with a few curious twists which have given the specialty an arcane reputation.

This chapter is mostly concerned with the law. But there is no point in knowing the law unless one can get to court to argue it. It is therefore necessary to say something about access to justice, as Lord Woolf would put it.

## Running clinical negligence claims for claimants

Clinical negligence work is much more of a closed shop than it used to be. Most actions are still publicly funded. The Legal Services Commission, which holds the purse strings for publicly funded cases, will only fund cases which are handled by firms of solicitors which hold a clinical negligence franchise. This is a good thing. Before Legal Aid franchising clinical negligence work could be, and was, done by any solicitor. Lots of the solicitors who had a go at it had an unerring instinct for the wrong end of the stick. They instructed the same counsel that they used for trippers and burglaries, and between them they brought, at colossal public expense and great emotional cost to their clients, lots of laughably unmeritorious claims. Claimants were often hopelessly and embarrassingly outgunned, in terms of legal firepower, by defendants. That has changed. The people who do claimant clinical negligence work now are generally competent, and many of them are outstanding.

The advent of conditional fee (no win no fee) agreements has, so far, had little impact on clinical negligence cases. If public funding for clinical negligence cases were abolished, conditional fee agreements certainly could not plug the gap. There are several reasons for this. The first is that in order to know whether one has even a shadow of a chance in a clinical negligence case, it is necessary to obtain expert medical advice. That is often very expensive. Few individuals, and only the larger firms, will be able to fund, highly speculatively, the costs of that initial investigation. The second is that it is crucial to safeguard against the possible liability for the other side's costs by taking out insurance which would cover those costs. But clinical negligence litigation is laced with uncertainties. Insurers like greater certainties than it is usually possible to give. This means that often, even in clinical negligence cases with a relatively high prospect of success, it will be impossible to get insurance at an economically viable cost.

## Running clinical negligence claims for defendants

The defendants' side is even more of a closed shop. Where the defendant is an NHS Trust or Health Authority, the litigation is controlled by the National Health Service Litigation Authority (NHSLA). This, frankly, is highly resented by many of the NHS bodies it represents. There are many reasons for this. Foremost amongst them is the perception that it second-guesses the lawyers instructed by the Trust or Health Authority, and fails to take properly into account the views of the clinicians who are in the frame. The NHSLA has a small panel of approved solicitors who do all the Trust and Health Authority work, and the NHSLA's own lawyers and claims handlers keep a very close eye on everything which those solicitors do. All major and a lot of trivial steps in the litigation have to have the express endorsement of the NHSLA. This has led to the criticism that the NHSLA causes duplication of work. Get them off the record, and a lot of the solicitors who do NHSLA work will tell you how bitterly they resent the Big Brother supervision of the NHSLA. The ethos at the NHSLA is very much an insurance one. Clinicians' reputations do not weigh heavily in the NHSLA's equations. They are interested in the bottom line. One question which is sometimes asked is: Which bottom line? The NHSLA's *raison d'être* is saving money. It came into existence because lots of people were worried about NHS spending on litigation. Its constant rhetoric is that costs must be saved. It has various devices for ensuring this. One of the major ones is to settle cases early, so reducing the time that the legal taxi meters tick. But many think that the rush to settle results in eminently fightable cases being settled, which itself encourages other claimants to have a go. The amount of costs per case might have reduced since the NHSLA assumed its mantle, but if the amount of damages paid out is factored into the financial equation, has the NHSLA really justified its existence? The NHSLA is certainly very reluctant to fight cases. There is, of course, some economic sense behind this. Trials are expensive events. But there is a common perception that this costs defendants dear. Assume that there is a cerebral palsy case which, if the claimant succeeds, will result in an award of damages of £3.5 million. Assume that the claimant has a 60 per cent chance of success. This means that he has a 40 per cent chance of failure. All too often the defendant's reasoning is simply: "We will probably fail. A trial will be expensive. We should offer a slightly discounted settlement – say £3 million." Is this really prudent? A trial might cost £50,000. If one views litigation as a casino, which is a very good way to view it, the entry fee is

£50,000. This is the price one has to pay to spin the wheel. Only by spinning the wheel can one avoid a liability of £3 million. The chances of avoiding it are 40 per cent. Most intelligent gamblers would pay the entry fee.

It is important to know that NHS Trusts and Health Authorities are not insured for clinical negligence. The economics of insurance forbid it. This means that the costs of litigation and awards of damages are paid out of the NHS budget. A typical award in a brain-damaged baby case would pay for several consultants or several dialysis machines.

The other important people on the defendants' side are the defence organisations: the Medical Defence Union, the Medical Protection Society, and the Medical and Dental Defence Union of Scotland. They get involved when the defendant is a general practitioner or where the act or default has occurred in the course of private practice. It is possible, but unusual and logistically foolish, for individual practitioners in NHS hospital practice to be sued. An agreement between the defence organisations and the NHS led to 'Crown Indemnity' – a carve up whereby the NHS shouldered all the burden of NHS hospital litigation in return for the defence organisations picking up the bill for GP's.

The defence organisations have traditionally been mutual societies rather than insurance companies. This meant that they had a discretion to indemnify rather than a contractual obligation to do so. In practice this discretion, for obvious reasons, was generally exercised in favour of indemnity. Traditionally, too, the defence organisations have been more responsive than insurers to non-financial considerations – notably the wish of the doctor to defend his reputation. There are signs, though, that this ethos is changing. Hard-nosed insurers are getting the upper hand.

## The elements of a claim for negligence

Just as in a negligence claim in any other arena, the claimant has to prove:

(a) that the defendant owed him a duty; and
(b) that there has been a breach of duty; and
(c) that the breach of duty has caused loss of a type recognised by the law of tort.

Each of these elements is considered in turn.

## When is a duty owed?
### *The general principle: A doctor can choose who he treats*

A doctor owes a duty to his patients. The law does not require any doctor to enter into a doctor-patient relationship with anybody. The classic example is the provision of "good Samaritan care". No doctor is compelled to attend an accident victim. He can walk by and let the patient suffer and die. His conscience will be his only judge. There is only a moral obligation to rush forward to the cry: "Is there a doctor in the house?"

It is sometimes, and wrongly, said that there is an exception to this in the case of general practitioners. They are under a duty to provide medical services to people in their geographical area. But a GP who goes to help an accident victim in his area is not compelled by the law of tort to assume a doctor-patient relationship with the victim. His contract with the Primary Care Trust asserts that he has a doctor-patient relationship with the victim anyway. The GP did not have to sign the contract which created that relationship.

## When is a patient a patient?

The general answer which follows from the above discussion is that a patient is a patient when the doctor decides that he is. But it is not quite as simple as that.

Although the courts have repeatedly and increasingly indicated that the law of negligence is a fluid organism, expanding to accommodate changes in society,[1] they have also been very conservative in imposing new duties on professionals. The general criteria for the imposition of a duty are set out in *Caparo Industries plc v. Dickman*,[2] which laid down the famous three-fold test: There will be a duty if the injury is foreseeable, the relationship between the claimant and the defendant is sufficiently proximate, and if it is just and reasonable to impose such a duty.

Although judges are obliged to consider these three elements separately, in practice decisions about the proximity of relationship are coloured by considerations of justice and reasonableness, which is fair enough.

If any general principle can be discerned in the cases about medical duties, it is that a duty will not be imposed unless the doctor has explicitly agreed to assume it. Contractual and tortious duties are, in this arena, usually found to be co-extensive.

Two examples illustrate this:

D1 was a building society. D2 was a GP engaged by D1 as a medical adviser. C applied for a job with D1. She filled in a medical questionnaire. D2 looked at the questionnaire, and concluded that C had sickle cell anaemia and was likely to have a lot of time off work. He told this to D1. D1 did not employ C. C said that D2 had negligently assessed the risk

---

1. See, for example, *X v. Bedfordshire County Council* [1995] AC 633.
2. [1990] 2 AC 605.

from sickle cell anaemia. D2 said that he did not owe C any duty, and accordingly it was irrelevant whether or not he was negligent. The Court of Appeal agreed with this. D2 owed a duty only to D1.[3]

D performed a vasectomy on A and told him that it had been successful and that he need take no future contraceptive precautions. Subsequently A met C, and told her that he was sterile. They started a sexual relationship and used no contraception. C became pregnant. She sued D. Her case was struck out: D owed C no duty.[4]

This is not to say that a duty cannot be owed to third parties of whose existence a doctor does not know. Consider the situation where X, a psychiatric patient, says that if he is released he would kill the first person he met outside the hospital. X's doctor, Y, knowing of the threat, nonetheless releases X. X keeps his promise and kills a stranger, Z, on the hospital steps. It may well be held that Y owed Z a duty. But the English courts are unlikely to go much further than this at the moment. They would be unlikely to impose a duty on Y in relation to all future potential victims of X, just as they would not impose a duty on D, in the example immediately above, to all future sexual partners of A. The existence of a duty in cases like these is likely to depend on an ascertainable (and probably numerically small) class of potential victims.[5]

This is as good a place as any to consider the rather special case of liability for psychiatric injury. This is a rapidly evolving area of the law of tort, but it is still dominated by the cases which

---

3. *Kapfunde v. Abbey National plc and Daniel* [1999] 2 Lloyd's Rep. Med. 48.
4. *Goodwill v. British Pregnancy Advisory Services* [1996] 2 All ER 161.
5. See *Palmer v. South Tees Health Authority* [1999] Lloyd's Rep. Med. 151.

followed the Hillsborough Disaster.[6] A lot of the confusion has arisen from frank judicial scepticism about psychiatric injury. The courts have tended to think that unless bones are broken or blood spilt, there is no real injury, and that the right approach to psychiatric devastation is tea and a stiff upper lip rather than compensation. But they are gradually realising that the boundary between the physical and the psychiatric is permeable or non-existent: the law is changing accordingly. Another policy consideration, however, will not go away: the courts are scared of opening the floodgates. However sympathetic one is to psychiatric injury, it has to be conceded that it is a lot less verifiable than physical injury, and a lot more common. There is a residual belief that the stiff upper lip should be actively encouraged, and that people should not be paid out for perceived moral weakness.

The Hillsborough cases distinguished between primary and secondary victims of a tort. The best way of analysing these is in terms of whether or not a duty is owed. There is no difficulty about primary victims. The ordinary principles, discussed above, adequately identify them. A primary victim is someone who could, foreseeably, have suffered physical injury. Generally, in medical cases, that will be a patient. Such a victim can recover damages for psychiatric injury even when there is no peg of physical injury on which to hang the claim. A secondary victim is one who was not actually present at the time that physical injury was possible, but who suffers psychiatric injury as a result of injury to another. A duty is only owed to such a claimant if the claimant is in a sufficiently close relationship of love and affection to the injured person, is present at the event or its immediate aftermath and sees

---

6.  *Alcock v. Chief Constable of South Yorkshire* [1992] 1 AC 310 and *White v. Chief Constable of South Yorkshire* [1998] 3 WLR 1509. See also *Page v. Smith* [1996] AC 155.

or hears the event or its aftermath.

Issues of liability to potential secondary victims commonly arise in medical law, and the courts are increasingly sympathetic to claimants. A typical example would be a father watching the delivery of his dead child - dead as a result of clinical negligence.[7] Judicial sympathy is particularly evident in the increasingly elastic construction of the notion of 'immediate aftermath'.

## *The position in NHS hospitals*

The general principles still obtain in hospitals, although it sometimes does not seem like that. An individual doctor is under no tortious duty to anyone other than his patients. He can choose, so far as the law of tort is concerned, whom to accept as his patient. If a patient walks into a clinic and demands treatment from Dr. A, Dr. A will be safe from allegations of negligence if he says no, even if there are no good clinical reasons for saying no. He may not be safe from allegations of breach of contract, but those could only be levelled by his employer, not by the patient. What amounts in a hospital setting to an assumption of a doctor-patient relationship depends on the facts. The issue is very rarely debated in the courts. It does not have to be, because there is no advantage to the patient in suing an individual clinician when, as discussed below, he can sue the NHS Trust in charge of the hospital instead.

The debate could only arise in the context of allegedly negligent omissions. Where there is a negligent professional act, almost by definition a doctor-patient relationship has been created. In the case of a negligent omission, the courts would no doubt be ready to imply the assumption of a doctor-patient relationship in most emergency situations where the doctor's whole *raison d'être*

---

7. As in *Tredgett v. Bexley Health Authority* [1994] 5 Med LR 178.

is the provision of emergency care. The courts might well say that the very fact that the doctor turned up for duty that day and was sitting round, knowingly bearing the burden of responding to emergency calls, meant that he entered into the relationship with anyone who needed truly emergency care. The position is logically the same for non-emergency patients, but the policy considerations which drive judicial decisions about the imposition of tortious duties would probably restrict the ambit of the logic to blue-light situations.

NHS Trusts have a statutory duty to provide medical, surgical and nursing care. The duty is contained in lots of bits of subordinate legislation, but the parent of all that legislation is the National Health Service Act 1977. Section 1 says that the Secretary of State for Health has a:

> *"duty to continue the promotion ... of a comprehensive health service designed to secure improvement (a) in the physical and mental health of the people of those countries, and (b) in the prevention, diagnosis and treatment of illness, and for that purpose to provide or secure the effective provision of services in accordance with this Act."*

Section 3(1) is more explicit about what performance of this duty involves:

> *"It is the Secretary of State's duty to provide ... to such extent as he considers necessary to meet all reasonable requirement:*
> *(a) hospital accommodation;*
> *(b) other accommodation for the purpose of any service provided under this Act;*
> *(c) medical, dental, nursing and ambulance services;*
> *(d) such other facilities for the care of expectant mothers and nursing mothers and young children as*

he considers are appropriate as part of the health service;

(e) such facilities for the prevention of illness, the care of persons suffering from illness and the after-care of persons who have suffered from illness as he considers are appropriate as part of the health service;

(f) such other services as are required for the diagnosis and treatment of illness."

This is all laudable but vague stuff. None of it has the distinctive smell of an actionable statutory duty. There have been some wildly optimistic efforts to persuade the courts otherwise – to persuade them to say that the Secretary of State is liable for damages for a failure to perform these duties, but they have all failed.[8] The efforts amounted to invitations to the court to act as arbiters of the reasonableness of the Secretary of State's decisions. The invitations were declined, the courts saying that they could not interfere unless the decision was so unreasonable as to be frankly irrational.[9] The courts pointed out that the responsible deployment of funds involved weighing competing claims from endless would-be beneficiaries. A government department was far better placed to do that than a court. Similar problems face applicants in judicial review proceedings who say that an NHS Trust should have spent money on what the applicant wanted.

So as a starting point for a claim in negligence, the duties under the National Health Service Act are important, but a

---

8. See *R. v. Secretary of State for Social Services, ex parte Hincks* (1992) 1 BMLR 93; *R. v. Secretary of State for Health, ex parte Walker* (1992) 3 BMLR 32; *R. v. Central Birmingham Health Authority, ex parte Collier*, unreported, 1988.
9. *Associated Provincial Picture Houses Ltd v. Wednesbury Corporation* [1948] 1 KB 223.

claimant needs to go further. It is usual for "particulars of claim" in a clinical negligence claim against a Trust to start by stating that the Trust owes a duty, pursuant to the 1977 Act and subsequent and subordinate legislation, to provide medical, surgical, nursing and ancillary staff.[10] The subsequent allegations of negligence are generally framed as allegations of vicarious liability. They assert that the employees of the Trust did not do properly the job entrusted to them, and that the Trust has to pick up the bill for their failure. It is worth noting, though, that there are often, in practice, disguised claims for inadequate resources which are probably best analysed as a breach of the (non-actionable) duty under the 1977 Act or as a criticism of the decisions of Trust management about the allocation of funds. Such claims might appear as: 'There was no CTG monitor available' or 'There was a delay of five hours before the claimant was taken to the operating theatre.' It is very rare to see defendants respond to such allegations with the riposte: 'It is regrettable that there are not infinite resources in the NHS, but that sad fact does not ground an action in damages' – a riposte which the authorities would allow them to make.

## Contractual duties

For most practical purposes clinical negligence lawyers can forget about these. It is not that contractual duties do not exist – all private medicine and surgery is performed pursuant to such duties – but that they rarely add anything to the parallel duty owed in tort. The courts have been very reluctant to imply a duty in contract which goes beyond the duty imposed by the common law of negligence.

That said, there are sometimes arguments about contractual duties. The commonest example is plastic surgery. A claimant will

---

10. An example of such Particulars of Claim appears in Appendix 1.

classically say: "The surgeon promised me a perfect chin. It was a term of the contract that I got a perfect chin. Instead I got this. That is a breach of contract." The usual response of judges, however, is to say that it was a term of the contract that the surgeon would use, in counselling about the possible outcome and in aiming for the desired result, the skill and care reasonably to be expected of a competent surgeon of the professed expertise of the relevant surgeon. This amounts to saying that the surgeon is contractually bound not to be tortiously negligent in his pre-operative advice or in the performance of the operation.

## The standard of care and proving breach
### The Bolam test: General

This is where the ubiquitous *Bolam* test comes in.[11] The *Bolam* test gets its name from the direction of McNair J to the jury in *Bolam v. Friern Hospital Management Committee*.[12] It is both a rule of substantive law (stating what amounts to acceptable professional practice), and a rule of evidence (stating how one proves that the requisite standard has or has not been met) – hence the heading of this section.

It is best stated in negative terms. A doctor has not been negligent if what he has done would be (and will in the witness box be) endorsed by a responsible body of professional opinion in the relevant specialty.

One does not decide that a body of opinion is responsible by counting heads. There may be only a couple of pioneers at the frontier of medicine or surgery who would do things (or be capable of doing things) in the way that a particular defendant has done.

---

11. (1992) 175 CLR 479.
12. [1957] 1 WLR 582.

That does not make the defendant irresponsible, although it does mean that the court would look particularly closely at the counselling about risks and benefits which that defendant had given. To hold otherwise would be to strangle medical innovation.

That said, though, the courts tend to be conservative. They may pillory a clinician for being too ambitious: they will not damn him for being too dull.

The *Bolam* test has been abused by defendants and by judges. It used to be possible for a seriously negligent defendant to escape liability by getting into the witness box, at a handsome hourly fee plus lunch, someone in the relevant specialty with a smart suit and a Harley Street address who had miraculously escaped censure by the GMC during the course of an undistinguished professional life, to say not that he would have done things in the way that the defendant did them, but that he once met someone at the third tee who did things that way. Those days are gone. They were ushered out by the notorious case of *Bolitho v. City and Hackney Health Authority*.[13] *Bolitho* generated hysteria in the medico-legal world. Thousands of passionate words were written on it, saying how radically it had remodelled the legal landscape. This was an overreaction. All that it did was to put in italics the word "responsible" in the *Bolam* test. The word itself had always been there. It was up to counsel for the claimant to insist that it was italicised: sadly, until *Bolitho*, counsel never did.

The key passage in *Bolitho* is in the speech of Lord Browne-Wilkinson. He said:

> *"... in cases of diagnosis and treatment there are cases where, despite a body of professional opinion sanctioning the defendant's conduct, the defendant can properly be held liable*

---

13. [1998] AC 232.

> *for negligence ... In my judgment that is because, in some cases, it cannot be demonstrated to the judge's satisfaction that the body of opinion relied upon is reasonable or responsible.*"[14]

This passage is too often cited as the ratio of *Bolitho*. This is the one which caused all the excitement. On its face it is frightening for clinicians. It seems to say that it is in order for a lay judge whose only knowledge of biology comes from a pre-war prep school memory of a pithed frog, to reject as irresponsible a time-hallowed, textbook-enshrined medical practice. It does not sit easily with some things which have been said in the past. Two examples demonstrate this: both come from Lord Scarman.

> *"... There is seldom any one answer exclusive of all others to problems of professional judgment. A court may prefer one body of opinion to the other, but that is no basis for a conclusion of negligence."*[15]

> *" ... the law imposes the duty of care; but the standard of care is a matter of medical judgment."*[16]

But Lord Browne-Wilkinson did not stop there. Lots of the hysterical fears should be laid to rest by reading what he went on to say - making it clear that he was merely expounding the word "responsible", and not saying anything new.

> *"In the vast majority of cases the fact that distinguished experts in the field are of a particular opinion will demonstrate the reasonableness of that opinion. In particular,*

---

14. At 243.
15. *Maynard v. West Midlands Regional Health Authority* [1984] 1 WLR 634, at 638.
16. *Sidaway v. Bethlem Royal Hospital Governors* [1985] 1 All ER 643, at 649.

*where there are questions of assessment of the relative risks and benefits of adopting a particular medical practice, a reasonable view necessarily presupposes that the relative risks and benefits have been weighed by the experts in forming their opinions. But if, in a rare case, it can be demonstrated that the professional opinion is not capable of withstanding logical analysis, the judge is entitled to hold that the body of opinion is not reasonable or responsible. I emphasise that in my view it will very seldom be right for a judge to reach the conclusion that views genuinely held by a competent medical expert are unreasonable. The assessment of medical risks and benefits is a matter of clinical judgment which a judge would not normally be able to make without expert evidence ... it would be wrong to allow such assessment to deteriorate into seeking to persuade the judge to prefer one of two views both of which are capable of being logically supported. It is only where a judge can be satisfied that the body of expert opinion cannot be logically supported at all that such opinion will not provide the bench-mark by reference to which the defendant's conduct falls to be assessed ... "*[17]

The judges have, by and large, not seen *Bolitho* as an opportunity to second-guess the experts. At least at appellate level the *Bolam* test is as the *Bolam* test was.[18]

The real effect of *Bolitho* is on legal practitioners and the experts they instruct. Experts tend to be less confidently pompous. They do not say, as they used to: "I've got a big private practice, and I do it that way, so there's an end of the matter." If they are

---

17. At 243.
18. A good example is *Calver v. Westwood Veterinary Group* [2001] Lloyd's Rep. Med. 20, a failed attempt by the author to persuade the Court of Appeal that *Bolitho* was more a revolution than a polite discussion.

instructed by half-competent lawyers, they will not be allowed to get away with that. Their reports, these days, need to bristle with foot-notes before they can be served. The lawyers are less coy about cross-examining the experts on the journals. Every position taken needs to be supported by logic and the literature.

## *The Bolam test, evidence-based medicine, and clinical guidelines*

Probably this was going to happen anyway, regardless of *Bolitho*. That is because of the galloping progress of evidence-based medicine. Increasingly, there are right and wrong answers in medicine: answers which are supported by the literature and answers which are not. An answer which goes against all the literature will not be a responsible one, however often it is adopted by consultants and however stoutly it is defended. Of course the literature does not always speak with one voice. The validity of studies can always be criticised: statistics often equivocate. But increasingly there is consensus. Where there is debate about what amounts to a responsible conclusion on the literature, it may be that the real gladiators in future clinical negligence cases will be the statisticians, sparring about the statistical significance of the results which underpin the seminal studies.

Individual clinicians cannot be expected to evaluate all relevant studies themselves, but they can be expected to take heed of what their Trusts and the relevant professional bodies say, in clinical guidelines and protocols, about the consensus of the literature. The rapid march of evidence-based medicine is reflected in the increasing importance of such guidelines.

Clinicians are worried about protocols because they think that failure to follow them will necessarily connote negligence. This is nonsense. The *Bolam* test does not cease to apply simply because a protocol has been drafted.

The courts are, however, tending to regard clinical guidelines as indicators of accepted clinical practice. Of course they are not evidence in themselves of good or any practice. Unless produced by an expert they are simply inadmissible. There cannot procedurally be mere trials by protocol.

In *Loveday v. Renton*[19] Stuart-Smith LJ said:

> "... *so far as the Plaintiff seeks to rely on the contraindications as evidence of the opinions of experts not called as witnesses ... this evidence is inadmissible in law. The reason for this is obvious; it is not known who holds the opinion or basis for it; and the evidence is not tested in cross-examination before the court. It is hearsay. But it is part of the medical literature in the case, experts are entitled to and have commented on it; and in particular have drawn inferences as to the incidence of the vaccine associated cases in relation to the observance or non-observance of the contraindications.*"[20]

He went on:

> "*the evidence contained in the contraindications against pertussis vaccination, published from time to time in this country by the DHSS and similar bodies in other countries, cannot be relied upon as though it was evidence of qualified experts not called as witnesses, that the vaccine in fact causes permanent brain damage.*"[21]

In *Ward v. Ritz Hotel (London)*[22] the Court considered the relevance of the British Standards' Institution recommendations in the context of an accident at work:

---

19. [1990] 1 Med LR 117.
20. At p.30.
21. At p.182.
22. [1992] PIQR 315 at 327.

*"[the British Standards] represent the consensus of professional opinion and practical experience as to the sensible safety precautions. How much weight they attach to them is shown by the words which I have quoted used in the laying down of the Standard. I would also accept and agree with the words used by HHJ Newey QC sitting as an Official Referee in The Board of Governors for the Hospitals for Sick Children v McLaughlin & Harvey plc 19 Con L.R. 25, 93:*

*"British Standards Codes of Practice are not legal documents binding upon engineers or upon anyone else, but they reflect the knowledge and expertise of the profession at the date when they were issued. They are guides to the engineer and in my view they also provide strong evidence as to the standard of the competent engineer at the date when they were issued ... "*

The English courts' approach to clinical guidelines is illustrated well in the following three cases:

(a) *Re C (A Minor) (Medical Treatment)* [23]
The High Court considered the status of the guidance issued by the Royal College of Paediatrics and Child Health entitled *"Withholding or Withdrawing Lifesaving Treatment in Children, a Framework for Practice.* It concluded:

*"So it is clear that what is being proposed by the doctors has the support of the Royal College of Paediatrics and Child Health who considered the wide field of these matters in their meetings which led to the publication of that document."*

---

23. [1998] Lloyd's Rep. Med.1.

(b) *Airedale NHS Trust v. Bland* [24]
   The House of Lords considered guidance issued by the Medical Ethics Committee of the BMA in relation to patients in a permanent vegetative state. Lord Goff concluded:

   *"... if a doctor treating a PVS patient acts in accordance with the medical practice now being evolved by the Medical Ethics Committee of the BMA, he will be acting with the benefit of guidance from a responsible and competent body of relevant professional opinion, as required by the Bolam test."* [25]

(c) *Early v. Newham HA* [26]
   The High Court considered the status of locally issued guidelines relating to failed intubation, and concluded:

   *"It is, of course, common for attacks to be made against the medical profession but having heard Dr McAteer describing how, in relation to this procedure, it was put before the division of anaesthesia in the hospital, all consultants at Newham together, there are about ten of them there, seven or eight of whom are consultants who then decided that this was the proper procedure to follow and minutes of the discussion were kept. I find it somewhat unfortunate that Professor Robinson should suggest that those consultants and the drill that they adopted was nevertheless such that no reasonably competent medical authority could have adopted it."* [27]

Generally, concordance with Department of Health or professional organisational standards, or reasonably well-considered local

---

24. [1993] 4 Med LR 39.
25. At p.61.
26. [1994] 5 Med LR 214.
27. At p. 216.

protocols is likely to exculpate. If a protocol does exist and it is not followed because a clinician has exercised independent clinical judgment and adopted an alternative method which would be *Bolam* defensible, he will escape liability. The position of para-medical personnel may be rather different. They may not be expected to exercise clinical judgment where such exercise would result in them failing to follow a protocol. Where they fail to follow a protocol, but nonetheless what they do would be endorsed by some body of responsible medical opinion, they might nonetheless be liable.

The relevance of clinical guidelines has been considered in detail here because of their intimate and complex relationship with what amounts to responsible clinical practice. Bigger books than this dissect up the duty of doctors in more detail. Ultimately, though, the only question to be asked is the general *Bolam* one: would a responsible body of medical opinion rubber-stamp the doctor's conduct? There is only one further general point which needs to be made (that doctors are judged according to the standard they set themselves), and three areas of difficulty which need to be explored (consent, resources and alternative medicine).

## Compliance with self-imposed standards

The law judges doctors by the standard that they hold themselves out as having. If you are a GP and decide to undertake cardiac bypass surgery in your kitchen, it is no use saying: "I did this surgery as well as any competent GP, having only kitchen implements at his disposal, would have done." You will be judged by the standard of a competent heart surgeon in a reasonably well equipped operating theatre.

## Consent

Lord Browne-Wilkinson inserted a curious caveat into his notorious speech in *Bolitho*. He restricted his endorsement of the *Bolam* test to "cases of diagnosis and treatment." The significance of this reservation to cases brought in negligence and based on inadequate counselling/taking of consent are discussed in detail in the chapter on Consent.

## Resources

Medicine is not practised in an economic vacuum. It can be put brutally: keep X alive, and Y and Z, who need his bed, will die. So what should be done?

The law has been coy and cowardly about this. In case after case the judges have called for a basin and washed their hands. But the blood of Y and Z is on someone's hands. The ethical debate is the old one: should we be ruthless utilitarians, subjugating all other values to the demands of the actuaries? Should a QALY-supported argument trump all others? Clinicians and health service managers do not have the luxury of declining to engage in that debate. But the judges do.

The law about the allocation of medical resources is a mess. It is painfully dislocated from the wider law relating to the provision of medical treatment. It is clear that the European Convention on Human Rights speaks, in this area as in many others, with too equivocal a voice to help: see, for example, *R (on the application of Yvonne Watts) v. (1) Bedford Primary Care Trust (2) Secretary of State for Health*.[28] The courts acknowledge that not all desirable treatment can always be provided, even where that treatment may

---

28. [2004] Lloyd's Rep. Med. 113.

be life-saving. The best and most heartbreaking example is the Child B case: see *R. v. Cambridge Health Authority, ex parte B*.²⁹ The courts will even endorse policies which decree that certain types of treatment will not be provided, provided that those policies have been made in a rational way. Thus it would be lawful to refuse to pay for any gender reassignment surgery if the policy of refusal is justified in a transparent and logical way: see *North West Lancashire Health Authority v. A, D and G*.³⁰ But a policy which forbade the provision of essential, obviously life-saving treatment for designated classes of patients for whom that treatment was in their best interests would be likely to be looked at much more critically. There is a clear presumption that it is in patients' best interests to continue to live. That presumption will operate wherever it cannot be shown that continued life is intolerable.³¹ The public law considerations which lead the courts quite readily to rubber stamp policies would be likely to give way to the more fundamental considerations of "best interests" where the application of a policy would be likely to cause the death of identifiable individuals. The Child B case is likely to be regarded as distinguishable on the grounds that the proposed treatment might have been, but probably would not have been, life saving. If, in an individual case, treatment would probably prolong life, then there is probably a duty in that case to provide it. And probably a policy which purported to usurp the individual decision-making process in such cases would be deemed unlawful however

---

29. [1995] 1 WLR 898.
30. [2000] 1 WLR 977.
31. See *R (on the application of Burke) v. General Medical Council* [2004] EWHC 1879 (Admin); *In Re J (A Minor) (Wardship: Medical Treatment)* [1991] Fam 33; *In Re B (A Minor) (Wardship: Medical Treatment)* [1981] 1 WLR 1421. *In Re C (A Minor) (Wardship: Medical Treatment)* [1990] Fam. 26; *Re R (Adult: Medical Treatment)* [1996] 2 FLR 99; *A National Health Service Trust v. D* [2000] 2 FLR 677.

impeccable the reasoning behind that policy was.

If the law should be internally consistent, all this is obviously and grossly unsatisfactory. Any first year philosophy undergraduate would make short work of it. And there are practical problems too. If the existence of an obligation to provide life saving treatment really turns on the probability of the success of that treatment, lives hang on an individual clinician's often arbitrary assessment of the likelihood of success. And is it really ethical to withhold treatment which has a 49 per cent chance of avoiding death, but be compelled to provide treatment which has a 51 per cent chance of avoiding it? Few would disagree that it would be lawful to have a policy which (for example), refused (on statistical, clinical grounds) coronary bypass surgery to smokers. But it is clearly in the best interests of many individual smokers to have bypass surgery. How does that square with the principle that the best interests of the individual prevail? It simply doesn't. It would certainly be unlawful to have a policy which permitted the withdrawal of nutrition and hydration from a PVS patient without the sanction of the court (see *Bland*) – a fact which leads to the deep irony that insensate patients might, so far as resources are concerned, be in a better position than sensate ones. And all this is without beginning to mention the uncomfortable fact with which this discussion started – the fact that to treat X may mean the death of Y.

The courts are rightly reluctant to interfere with the making of clinical decisions in individual cases, and with the making of policy about how clinical decisions should be made. But if the courts themselves create dilemmas, they should be ready to help to resolve them. That basin has to be thrown away. Judicial hands have to get dirty.

## *Alternative medicine*

Alternative medicine has grown massively in recent years. Like everyone else, alternative practitioners sometimes make mistakes, and some of those mistakes cause damage. But how does one establish whether a mistake is negligent? Does the *Bolam* test apply? If so, is the alternative practitioner to be judged by the standard of responsible alternative practitioners, or by the standard of responsible orthodox practitioners undertaking treatment of similar conditions?

These questions were considered in *Shakoor v. Situ.*[32] The defendant there was a qualified practitioner of traditional Chinese herbal medicine ("TCHM"). He was a member of an association called the Register of Chinese Herbal Medicine, whose members are subject to a code of ethics and need to have demonstrated by examination certain minimum standards of competence. The claimant was the widow of a man who had attended the defendant seeking treatment for benign lipomata. The defendant had prescribed a traditional herbal remedy. The deceased suffered an idiosyncratic reaction to the remedy and died. It was agreed that the herbal remedy was the cause of death.

The claimant did not call evidence from a practitioner of TCHM, but instead relied on a consultant dermatologist and a consultant physician and hepatologist. She contended (curiously, in light of the fact that no general practitioner was called) that the standard required of the defendant was that required of an orthodox general practitioner, and that there was a breach of duty here because an orthodox general practitioner would have known of warnings in the orthodox medical literature about idiosyncratic reactions to herbal medicines and would either not have prescribed the medicines at all or would have given such a stern warning about the risk of an idiosyncratic reaction that the deceased would not have taken the medicines.

---

32. [2001] 1 WLR 410.

On the facts the claimant failed to establish that an orthodox general practitioner would have been negligent in failing to notice the warnings in the literature or that, if he had noticed them, would have concluded that prescription was too dangerous or that prescription necessitated a warning which would have led to the medicines not being taken. The interest of the case lies in what was said about the standard of care.

The judge said that:

> "... when a court has to adjudicate on the standard of care given by an alternative medical practitioner it will, pace Bolitho v. City and Hackney Health Authority [1998] AC 232, often (perhaps invariably) not be enough to judge him by the standard of the ordinary practitioner "skilled in that particular art"; it will often be necessary to have regard to the fact that the practitioner is practising his art alongside orthodox medicine; the court will need to consider whether the standard of care adopted by the alternative practitioner has taken account of the implications of this fact ... "[33]

There were two main reasons for this conclusion. First, one could not ignore the fact that patients of alternative practitioners chose, for whatever reason, to reject orthodox medicine. Why should such patients be entitled later to complain that they did not receive treatment which would be endorsed by responsible orthodox practitioners?

Second, one could not ignore the fact that this country has laws which govern the standards of medical care and are in place for the protection of its citizens. The need for protection does not evaporate as soon as one leaves orthodox medicine behind.

---

33. At p.417.

Alternative practitioners, having chosen to practise in this country, must accept that some of these protective laws may influence their practice. The judge made this point by observing that had the defendant's qualification in China been recognised in England so as to allow him to practice orthodox medicine here, he would not escape a finding of negligence in England by showing that he had complied with the standard of care expected in Beijing, if the standard expected in Beijing was lower.

Thus a claimant can succeed in an action against an alternative practitioner for negligent prescription either by calling an expert from the alternative specialty in question to show that the defendant has failed to exercise the skill and care expected of a responsible alternative practitioner, or by proving that "... the prevailing standard of skill and care "in that art" is deficient in this country having regard to risks which were not and should have been taken into account." The practitioner has a duty to take reasonable steps to ensure (the judge in fact said simply "to ensure", but it is clear from the context that he did not mean this) that the remedy prescribed is not actually or potentially harmful. He must recognise that adverse reactions to such remedies are likely to have been recorded in the orthodox medical literature, and must take reasonable steps to satisfy himself that there have been no adverse reports in that literature which ought to affect the use he makes of the remedy. The practitioner is not required to take a range of relevant journals himself: *"It should be enough if he subscribes to an 'association' which arranges to search the relevant literature and promptly report any material publication to him. The relevant literature will be that which would be taken by an orthodox practitioner practising at the level of specialty at which the alternative practitioner holds himself out. If he does not subscribe to such an association the practitioner will not have discharged his duty to inform himself properly and may act at his peril.*"[34]

*Shakoor* provides a realistic and practical framework for considering the liability of alternative practitioners for allegedly negligent treatment. The Judge explicitly left open the question of whether the standard of diagnostic skill expected by alternative practitioners should be judged by the principles he outlined. The policy considerations which make it unacceptable that alternative practitioners should be judged merely by the standards of alternative practitioners are likely to cause the courts to insist that in the realm of diagnosis alternative practitioners conform more nearly to orthodox medicine.

## Will *Bolam* survive the Human Rights Act?

When the Human Rights Act 1998 was enacted, lots of lawyers were reading the rites over *Bolam*. But *Bolam* is still with us. The dangers it faces in the context of clinical negligence litigation are more from the evolution of evidence-based medicine, as discussed above, rather than from the ECHR. And *Bolam* is really honoured, rather than abolished, by evidence-based medicine, since in future there may often be only one *Bolam* defensible answer.

The ECHR arguments against *Bolam* rest on Article 2, which states:

> "*1. Everyone's right to life shall be protected by law. No-one shall be deprived of his life intentionally save in the execution of a sentence of Court following his conviction of a crime for which this penalty is provided by law.*"

The argument that *Bolam* and Article 2 cannot live together goes:

---

34. At p.417.

(a) Article 2 gives an absolute right to life.
(b) The *Bolam* test in effect asserts that there is no absolute right to life. A life can be lost without there being a remedy if a responsible body of medical opinion would have acted in a way which would have led to that loss. Article 2 has no room for such caveats.

This view is supposed to be supported by *Osman v. UK*,[35] in which it was said:

> *"Having regard to the nature of the right protected by Article 2, a right fundamental to the scheme of the Convention, it will be sufficient for an applicant to show that the authorities did not do all that could reasonably be expected of them to avoid the real and immediate risk to life of which they have or ought to have knowledge. This is a question which can only be answered in the light of all the circumstances of the case."*

Extrapolating from that, the anti-*Bolam*-ites say that inadequate medical treatment, absent negligence, grounds an Article 2 claim.

This extrapolation is nonsensical. The *Osman* formulation requires the court to enquire into what "could reasonably be expected of [the relevant doctors]." The English procedure for conducting that enquiry involves the *Bolam* test. The use of that test does not obviously fall foul of Article 2 or any other Article.

If the *Bolam* test goes, damages for clinical negligence go up and the resources available for patient care in the NHS go down. That consideration alone is likely to prompt the courts to say that the English procedural test falls within an acceptable "margin of appreciation", and therefore should survive.

---

35. [1999] 1 FLR 193.

Article 2 challenges to *Bolam* are more robust in the area of consent to treatment and withdrawal of treatment. This issue is considered in detail in the chapter on the law of death.

## The burden and standard of proof

This is easy. The burden of proving the case rests always and only on the claimant. The standard of proof is the balance of probabilities.

It sometimes used to be thought that the old rule of evidence, *res ipsa loquitur*, meant that where the facts screamed unequivocally that the defendant was liable, the burden of disproving negligence shifted to the defendant. This is not the case, if indeed it ever was. The notion that there was a special class of *res ipsa loquitur* cases to which special evidential rules applied met its end in *Plymouth & Torbay HA and Exeter & North Devon HA*.[36]

In *Ratcliffe* Hobhouse LJ said that:

> "[The maxim] *is no more than a convenient Latin phrase used to describe the proof of facts which are sufficient to support an inference that a defendant was negligent and therefore to establish a prima facie case against him ..."*[37]

All the talk about the shifting of evidential burdens of proof where the maxim applies has served only to confuse. Hobhouse LJ made the position clear:

> *"The burden of proving the negligence of the defendant remains throughout upon the plaintiff. The burden is on the*

---

36. [1998] PIQR P170.
37. At p.186.

*plaintiff at the start of the trial and absent an admission by the defendant is still upon the plaintiff at the conclusion of the trial. At the conclusion of the trial the judge has to decide whether upon all the evidence adduced at the trial he is satisfied upon the balance of probabilities that the defendant was negligent and that negligence caused the plaintiff's injury. If he is so satisfied he gives judgment for the plaintiff; if not, he gives judgment for the defendant."*[38]

This is the most trite law imaginable. But understand this, said the Court, and you understand the maxim. There is simply nothing more to be said about it. Hobhouse LJ hammered the point home hard, saying:

*"Whether or not the plaintiff has at some earlier stage relied upon a prima facie case does not alter this position. The plaintiff may or may not have needed to call evidence to establish a prima facie case. The admitted facts may suffice for that purpose ... Conversely, the defendant may have chosen to call no evidence, in which case the court will have to decide whether the evidence adduced by the plaintiff suffices to satisfy the court, in the absence of any evidence to contradict it, that the defendant was negligent and that his negligence caused the plaintiff's injury. In all these situations the task of the judge at the end of the trial is the same. The only difference is that he may be left without direct evidence as to what occurred and may have to act upon inferences to be drawn from incomplete evidence. Where the defendant is in a position to adduce evidence as to what occurred, but has refrained from doing so, the court will be more willing to draw inferences adverse to*

---

38. At p.186.

*the defendant than might otherwise be the case. Where the plaintiff is not in a position himself to give an account himself of what occurred and where the relevant situation was under the control of the defendant and the relevant facts are known to the defendant, the case may come fairly and squarely within the statement of Erle CJ ... But it does so because the facts proved have given rise to an inference that the defendant was negligent. Where there is direct evidence as to what occurred there is no need to rely upon inferences (Barkway v. South Wales Transport [1950] 1 All ER 392). There is no rule that a defendant must be liable for any accident for which he cannot give a complete explanation ... "*[39]

So, all the evidence available has to be considered. If the circumstances are such that the uncontradicted facts necessarily connote negligence then, unsurprisingly, the claimant will succeed if the defendant adduces no evidence. In such a case, though, the defendant will succeed if it gives an explanation of what has happened which is inconsistent with negligence, or by showing that it had exercised reasonable care: see *Delaney v. Southmead HA.*[40]

In *Ratcliffe* the first of these possible ways of preventing the inference being made was examined. Brooke LJ, adopting the ratio of *Bull v. Devon AHA*,[41] said:

*"The explanation must be a plausible one and not a theoretically or remotely possible one, but the defendant certainly does not have to prove that his explanation is more likely to be correct than any other. If the plaintiff has no other*

---

39. At p.187.
40. [1995] 6 Med LR 355.
41. [1993] 4 Med LR 117.

*evidence of negligence to rely on, his claim will then fail.*"[42]

## Causation
### *Introduction*

Causation is an integral part of the tort of negligence. The words "negligence" and "liability" are often used too loosely by lawyers to mean simply breach of duty. Proof of breach by itself is no good to a claimant.

Causation is very often the real battleground in clinical negligence claims. It is only common sense that if negligence has not caused damage the defendant should not pay, but causation defences often seem artificial and unfair to lay clients.

One warning. There are, in a way, two entirely different types of causation law. There is the law which deals with the question of whether the claimant has proved damage such that the tort of negligence is consummated; and there is the law dealing with the question of the amount of damages which are recoverable as a result of that consummated tort. It is not always easy to tell which type of law should be applied. The House of Lords itself sometimes has difficulty.

This chapter does not deal at all with the law relating to the assessment of damages. We are dealing here solely with the law of causation in the first sense.

### *The basic rule: The 'but-for' test*

The claimant generally has to show that but for the defendant's negligence he would probably have avoided the injury for which he claims.

---

42. At p.184.

This is quintessential expert witness territory. A lot of the life of a clinical negligence lawyer is spent trying to persuade doctors to say that on the balance of probabilities, had the negligence not occurred, the damage would not have occurred either. Or vice versa. Doctors hate this exercise, and very often do not understand it. There are two reasons for the confusion. First, doctors are used to making assertions about causation only if the assertion can be justified to a standard acceptable to the editors of medical journals. The standards demanded there are, to a lawyer, ridiculously high. Typically a confidence interval of 95 per cent is used. Many good doctors are coy about supporting a position on causation if the probabilities are very much less than this. Second, doctors live in the real world, and know that it is often impossible to squeeze all the complexity of medicine into the little statistical boxes that lawyers are so fond of. Often it will genuinely be impossible for a doctor to do better than "it might have done", but that is no good in the courts.

*Bolam* has a role in causation. If a clinician negligently fails to put himself in a position to treat a patient (for example by failing to answer a bleep), one then has to ask: What would have happened if the clinician had turned up? There will of course be great psychological pressure on the clinician to say that he would not have done whatever was necessary to avoid the damage. It was those considerations which led some[43] to say that one should presume that what would have been done is that which would have avoided the damage. But that is unsatisfactory. If that were the law, claimants effectively would be absolved from the need to prove causation at all in these "hypothetical causation" cases. The House

---

43. Notably Simon Brown LJ in the Court of Appeal in *Bolitho v. City and Hackney Health Authority, supra.*

of Lords in *Bolitho*[44] said that a claimant in such a situation can succeed in one of two ways. He can either show that the clinician who should have attended would in fact have acted in a way which would have avoided the damage, or he can show that not to have acted in a way which would have avoided the damage would be *Bolam*-negligent. This must be right. If *Bolam* determines breach of duty it is bound to have a place in hypothetical causation cases too.

## *Loss of a chance*

There is a mantra which used to be chanted religiously by medical negligence lawyers: "You cannot get damages for loss of a chance." It is not so often heard now. It was based on an important misunderstanding of the case of *Hotson v. East Berkshire Health Authority*.[45]

*Hotson* was about a little boy who fell out of a tree. He fractured his femur. He was taken to hospital where he was treated negligently. He developed avascular necrosis of his femoral head. The trial judge found that there was a better than evens chance that he would have developed that avascular necrosis even if he had been treated properly. The claimant argued, though, that he had nonetheless suffered damage. That damage, he said, was a significant (though less than 50 per cent) loss of a chance of avoiding the avascular necrosis. This, he contended, was damage of a sort which was, or should be recognised by the law of tort.

The Court of Appeal agreed with him. It noted that it was commonplace for lost chances to be compensated for in the law of

---

44. *Supra.*
45. [1987] AC 750.

contract. The classic example is *Chaplin v. Hicks*.[46] Miss Chaplin thought that she was very beautiful. She entered a beauty contest which was set up by the defendant's newspaper. By paying her entrance fee she had a contract with the paper. It was really a contract which gave her the chance of being branded Battersea's best. In breach of that contract the newspaper made an administrative error. Miss Chaplin was not summoned before the judges, and so lost that chance. She sued the newspaper, saying that she should be compensated for her lost chance. The court did not find that she would probably have won (she therefore failed the 'but-for') but nonetheless did give her damages representing the value of the lost chance.

The Court of Appeal in *Hotson* thought that the only distinction between *Chaplin's* case and *Hotson's* was that one was in contract and the other in tort. It explored thoroughly and coherently the policy and jurisprudential grounds for restricting claims for lost chances to contract. It found no reason in policy or logic for such a restriction. It noted that to draw such a distinction would be to create a bizarre anomaly. If *Hotson* had been a private patient, it would be very sensible to say that he had a contract with the hospital to give him the chance of avoiding the avascular necrosis (or at least take reasonable steps to give him the chance - which comes to the same thing). The principle in *Chaplin* would thus give him damages. It would be strange indeed, and surely contrary to public policy if, being an NHS patient who was the victim of precisely the same negligence, he got nothing.

The House of Lords in *Hotson* thought that it did not think that it needed to answer the question which advocates on both sides were asking it to answer, namely: Is a loss of a chance damage in the law of tort? It dodged the issue, saying that on the trial judge's

---

46. [1911] 2 KB 786.

finding of fact Master Hotson's femoral head was, as a matter of fact, doomed before the negligent doctors ever got their hands on him. The House thus left the real issue of the recoverability of loss of a chance open. The most definitive treatment of the issue remains the judgment of the Court of Appeal, which at least did think that it had to answer the question.

*Hotson*, wrongly, made it heretical to utter the words "loss of a chance" in most clinical negligence contexts. Some people, however, thought that the concept had a place in cases about non-diagnosis or negligent treatment of cancer cases. This idea came from *Judge v. Huntingdon Health Authority*,[47] a first instance decision whose ratio was legendarily obscure.

There were signs of judicial embarrassment about the flirting with lost chances in cancer cases:[48] At last, in *Gregg v. Scott*[49] the House grappled squarely with the issue. But, despite five speeches of great learning and intellectual honesty, some crucial questions remain. The ratio of *Gregg* is, on one level, clear. Where a claimant has suffered a loss of a chance of recovery as a result of medical negligence, but the chance is less than evens, he is not entitled to compensation for that lost chance. That will resolve many of the cases which have been waiting in the wings pending the decision. But *Gregg* is complex: it is likely to spur creative litigators to think of more imaginative ways of putting their claims.

The result in *Gregg* produces a result which many think is intuitively unjust. Imagine that a patient has cancer. He goes to his doctor at a stage when he has a 45% chance of recovery. The doctor negligently says that the condition is benign. The necessary treatment is delayed for months. When the correct diagnosis is

---

47. (1996) 6 Med. LR 223.
48. See, *Taylor v. West Kent Health Authority* [1997] 8 Med LR 25, which seemed to rehabilitate the straightforward 'but-for' test in cancer cases.
49. [2005] UKHL 2.

finally made the prospects of recovery are nil. Should the diminished chance of recovery not sound in damages? It should not, said the majority in *Gregg* (Lords Hoffmann and Phillips and Lady Hale). There were passionate dissents from Lords Nicholls and Hope.

The facts in *Gregg* were not so simple. The claimant had non-Hodgkin's lymphoma. His doctor negligently diagnosed a benign lipoma. The judge found that the negligent delay reduced the claimant's chance of 10 year survival from 42 per cent at the date of the relevant consultation to 25 per cent at the time of trial. It was therefore not possible to conclude, on the balance of probabilities, that earlier treatment would have affected the chance of 10 year survival. The claim therefore failed. The Court of Appeal, by a majority, agreed.

The claimant had two lines of argument. First, he said, no novel question about the recoverability of damages for a loss of chance arose at all. It was common ground that the delay caused some spread of cancer cells which could and should have been avoided. That spread was physical damage in the conventional sense. The tort was fully consummated: there was a breach of duty, and that breach had caused loss. He was, therefore, entitled to succeed. The only remaining question was how much the claim was worth. Once one was in the realm of quantification there was nothing unusual about the idea of damages for a lost chance. Valuing the lost chance might be practically tricky, but it was not conceptually demanding. The House referred to this as the "quantification argument."

The second argument was the undiluted loss of a chance argument. This asserted that a lost chance was real loss and should be recognised as such by the law.

Lawyers from outside the personal injury world might well wonder what all the fuss is about. Loss of an opportunity is commonly the ground of claims in both contract and tort. Little Miss Chaplin was entitled to damages to compensate her for the loss of her chance.[50] It was not necessary for the judge to decide that probably she would have outshone everyone else on the catwalk. When a solicitor fails to serve a claim in time, the claimant in the subsequent solicitors' negligence proceedings does not have to prove that his original claim would probably have succeeded: see *Kitchen v. Royal Air Force Association*.[51] The principle obtains in claims framed in tort as well as contract: see *Spring v. Guardian Assurance plc*.[52]

The common law of causation and quantification has rested heavily on the (usually common sensical) distinction between past facts and future prospects. Generally, when one is dealing with past facts, the balance of probabilities test is workable. And generally, in dealing with future prospects, it is not. Recognising this, the courts are happy to abandon their traditional devotion to the balance of probabilities when assessing future prospects, substituting, and working happily with, the notion of lost chances.[53] Such "future prospects" questions commonly go to the issue of quantification, and where they do they do not raise the spectre of the substantive law question of whether a lost chance is real damage.

But the rationale behind this distinction fails when confronted with hypothetical situations, such as arise in every case of failure to diagnose. A hypothetical past "fact" (such as how much a cancer would have spread if a claimant had had the treatment he should have had, but did not have) is just as uncertain as a hypothetical

---

50. *Chaplin v. Hicks, supra.*
51. [1958] 1 WLR 563.
52. [1995] 2 AC 296.
53. See, for instance, *Mallett v. McMonagle* [1970] AC 166 and *Davies v. Taylor* [1974] AC 207.

future prospect. And yet the law demands proof of it on the balance of probabilities – a demand it refuses to make of future prospects on the very ground that such prospects are uncertain in precisely the same way as hypothetical past "facts" are.

Lord Nicholls saw this as a powerful reason for allowing the appeal. If a doctor's negligence forces a claimant to frame his claim in terms of hypothetical past facts, is it really fair to allow the doctor to take refuge in the imponderables of pathology and require the claimant to prove his case on the balance of probabilities? And anyway, he said, to require this sort of proof makes the law look medically naïve. Diseases do not read even the basic medical text books, let alone tables of prognostic statistics. Surely the law which deals with the consequences of failing to diagnose those diseases should not behave as if they do. Medicine is throbbing with uncertainties; to pretend that its vagaries can be reduced to reliable lists of percentages is not just scientifically laughable; it is downright unjust.

This objection, though, did not move the majority.

The quantification argument was, on its face, powerful. It persuaded Latham LJ in the Court of Appeal. But it foundered in the House of Lords. Lord Hoffmann said that it begged the question raised in the second argument – namely, whether a loss of chance was compensable. And Lord Hoffmann and Lady Hale pointed out that, before one gets to the stage of quantification, the causal connection between a tort and consequential loss of any kind has to be proved on the balance of probabilities – precisely what could not be done here.

The speeches dealing with the true lost chance argument are full of the old tension between law and equity. Each judge would acknowledge that he or she was making a policy decision, and assert that justice was the ultimate end of the policy adopted. The majority thought that justice was best achieved by legal certainty;

the minority that justice demanded a relaxation of the old rules of causation to allow compensation in an individual case. The majority, in rejecting the loss of chance argument, found compelling the law's traditional insistence on the distinction between past facts and future prospects. Each acknowledged its shortcomings, but pragmatically said that since it was possible, without very strenuous forensic gymnastics, to analyse every question of medical causation in terms of a lost chance, to depart from the old rules would be to deprive the law of medical negligence of some important control mechanisms. Although the term was only used, disparagingly, by Lord Nicholls, this was really a case all about floodgates. The analogy with (for example) claims against solicitors for the negligent conduct of litigation remains embarrassing. Lady Hale made some attempt to save face by noting the arguments which might justify distinguishing between the two classes of case, but she never said why she felt compelled to reject the analogy. The arguments are familiar to academic lawyers, and really do not wash. One example illustrates the point. It is sometimes said that financial loss type claims might better be viewed as the loss of a chance of obtaining a benefit, rather than losing a chance of avoiding a detriment. But the distinction, if real, is hardly attractive: one might think that it was more important to compensate for the latter than for the former.

Equity, for the majority, lay in certainty. The main equitable imperative was that people knew where they stood. And if that meant individual worthy claimants were sometimes sacrificed on the altar of the burden of proof, then that was a price worth paying. There might be situations where the conventional rules had to give way,[54] but such exotic exceptions served only to emphasise the general rules.

---

54. *Fairchild v. Glenhaven Funeral Services* [2003] 1 AC 32 is the classic example.

The philosophical foundations of those rules were articulated by Lord Hoffmann, at para.79:

> "... *the law regards the world as in principle bound by laws of causality. Everything has a determinate cause, even if we do not know what it is. The blood starved hip joint in Hotson, the blindness in Wilsher, the mesothelioma in Fairchild; each had its cause and it was for the plaintiff to prove that it was an act or omission for which the defendant was responsible ... The fact that proof is rendered difficult or impossible because no examination was made at the time, as in Hotson, or because medical science cannot provide the answer, as in Wilsher, makes no difference. There is no inherent uncertainty about what caused something to happen in the past or about whether something which happened in the past will cause something to happen in the future. Everything is determined by causality. What we lack is knowledge and the law deals with lack of knowledge by the concept of the burden of proof.*"

This is stern stuff. It will be beautiful music to the ears of insurers.

It is still possible, to the relief of many, to talk about the law of causation. Many wondered, in the light of *Fairchild (infra)*, and *Chester v. Afshar*,[55] whether causation was being drummed off the tortious stage by amorphous principles of fairness – principles so strident that they never stopped to ask whether it was fair to make someone pay for something he had not caused.

The dissenting speech of Lord Phillips is, to a large degree, a strict lesson in how to use and how not to use scientific statistics in the courts. All that he says about this survives the majority's rejection of his conclusion. The main point is an obvious one: the statistics applying to populations of which an individual is a

---

55. [2004] UKHL 41.

member can only be extrapolated with extreme causation and dozens of caveats to that individual. This is the first lesson any actuary learns, but the law has been slow to learn it. Lord Phillips' tutorial will make the courts more statistically literate.

So far as the compensability of lost chances is concerned, personal injury litigation seems to be rather stricter than other areas of the law, but arguments about lost chances will not be silent: they will just become rather more subtle.

The most encouraging news for claimants comes from Lady Hale. She said, in effect, that Mr. Gregg had got over-excited about lost chances and in that over-excitement had failed to take some less arcane but more promising points:

> *"... it cannot be said that the later pain, suffering and loss of amenity caused by the need for further treatment, and the associated loss of earnings and costs of care, were consequential on the injury caused by the negligence. Even if the initial treatment had led to remission, the need for further treatment and the relapses would have happened anyway because of the disease.*
>
> *Even on conventional principles, this does not necessarily mean that the claimant is not entitled to anything at all. The defendant is liable for any **extra** pain, suffering, loss of amenity, financial loss and loss of expectation of life which may have resulted from the delay. If, without the delay, the claimant would have achieved a longer gap before more radical treatment became necessary, then he should be entitled to damages to reflect the acceleration in his suffering. If the pain and suffering he would have suffered anyway was made worse by the anguish of knowing that his disease could have been detected earlier, then he should be compensated for that.*

*There is also the distinct possibility that the delay reduced his life expectancy in the following sense. It is possible that had he been treated when he should have been treated, his median life expectancy then would have been x years, whereas given the delay in treatment his median life expectancy from then is x minus y. This argument requires that the assessment of loss of life expectancy be based on median survival rates: ie those to be expected of half the relevant population at the particular time. If half the men with Mr Gregg's condition would have survived for x years or over with prompt treatment, and half would have survived for less than x years, then x is the median life expectancy of the group. If the same calculation of life expectancy from when he should have been treated is done in the light of the delay in treatment, the median life expectancy may have fallen. There might therefore be a modest claim in respect of the 'lost years'.*

*But none of this appears to have been explored before the judge. This was presumably because the focus before him had been on establishing that the claimant would otherwise have achieved a complete 'cure'. Ignoring for the moment the particular definition of cure adopted in the medical evidence, this would have entitled the claimant to far more in the way of loss of earnings and cost of care than would a claim for a modest reduction in median life expectancy"* (paras.205-208: original emphasis).

The boundaries of the future battleground are well sketched out in these paragraphs.

## Material contribution and multiple competing causes

The 'but-for' test is very simple. Life is not. The law recognises this, and has carved out some important but philosophically shaky exceptions.

Bonnington Castings v. Wardlaw[56] established that where the evidence does not enable the relative contribution of various factors (some innocent, at least one due to the defendant's default) a claimant will succeed in establishing causation if he proves on the balance of probabilities that the defendant's negligence has made a material contribution to his injury.

The House of Lords appeared to take Bonnington Castings further in McGhee v. NCB,[57] holding that there is no difference between a material contribution and a material increase in the risk of injury. Of course there is a distinction. Most commentators, until the case of Fairchild v. Glenhaven Funeral Services Ltd [58] regarded McGhee as eccentric in the extreme, and steamrollered into irrelevance by Wilsher v. Essex AHA, which made no secret of its disapproval of McGhee.[59] But the House of Lords in Fairchild has rehabilitated McGhee.

Fairchild made it clear that the 'but-for' test is the usual rule. It also recognised that there were some situations where its application could create injustices for claimants, and the rule in McGhee should be substituted. Because remedying those injustices created a risk of injustices to defendants, the situations where McGhee should apply were tightly circumscribed. Lord Rodger (with whom the other judges broadly agreed) said that the McGhee test should apply where:

"(i)   It is impossible for the claimant to prove exactly how his injury was caused.
(ii)   The defendant's wrongdoing has materially increased the risk that the claimant will suffer injury (creating a

---

56. [1956] AC 613.
57. [1973] 1 WLR 1.
58. [2002] 3 WLR 89.
59. [1988] AC 1074.

*material risk of injury to a class of persons is insufficient).*

(iii) *The defendant's conduct must have been capable of causing the claimant's injury.*

(iv) *The claimant's injury was caused by the eventuation of the kind of risk created by the defendant's wrongdoing. It is not enough that the claimant's injury could have been caused by a number of different events, only one of which is the eventuation of the risk created by the defendant's wrongful act or omission. By contrast, the principle does not apply where the claimant has merely proved that his injury could have been caused by a number of different events, only one of which is the eventuation of the risk created by the defendant's wrongful act or omission.*

(v) *The claimant must show that his injury was caused by an agency that operated in the same, or substantially the same, way as was involved in the defendant's wrongdoing.*

(vi) *The principle continues to apply and is not excluded where the other possible source of the claimant's injury is a similar wrongful act or omission of another person, or where it is a similar, but lawful, act or omission of the same defendant."*[60]

How, if at all, this will affect clinical negligence litigation, remains to be seen. The general consensus is that it will have little affect. That consensus was weakened for a few months by the House of Lords in *Chester v. Afshar*[61] (when it was wondered if the whole of

---

60. At para.170. The other judges broadly agreed with him about these criteria.
61. *Supra.*

the law of causation was crumbling) and then re-strengthened by the House in *Gregg v. Scott*[62] (which reinforced the general rules and made it clear that *Chester* and *Fairchild* are curious exceptions to those rules). It is possible, though, that some *Wilsher*-type situations, where there are multiple competing candidates for the post of cause, could be squeezed into the *Fairchild* criteria.[63] This could occur where a patient has been passed between several similarly negligent hospitals or clinicians, the negligence has materially increased a risk which eventuates, and it is scientifically impossible to attribute the damage to one or other of the defendants. The rule in *Fairchild* might make each of the negligent parties liable.

Generally though, *Fairchild* is likely to be deployed in clinical negligence cases more for its robust endorsement of the 'but-for' test than for its creation of intellectually exotic exceptions to the general rule. The courts will not forget that what *Fairchild* really does is to allow claimants to succeed when they have failed to prove causation in any meaningful sense.

**Product liability**

Damage is not always caused by negligent clinicians or negligent systems. Sometimes it is caused by dangerous products. If the injured person has a contract with the supplier of the dangerous product, it may be possible to bring proceedings against that person for the damage. But very often, in a medical context, there will be no such contract. It will often, also, be difficult or impossible to prove negligence on the part of anyone. In circumstances like this

---

62. *Supra.*
63. *Wilsher (supra)* said that where there are multiple competing causes, and the claimant cannot prove to the requisite standard that the guilty cause did materially contribute or in fact cause the injury, his action fails.

the law of consumer protection can sometimes help.

The Consumer Protection Act 1987[64] imposes strict liability for death, injury or damage to property,[65] on producers, manufacturers, suppliers, importers into the EU, and bodies that put their own brand on a product.[66] The Act gives several defences, including (most pertinently in a medical context), a "state of the art" defence. This means that there will be no liability for a defect which, given the state of scientific knowledge at the time of production, could not have been discovered.[67]

A "product" is defined very widely as any goods or electricity, and includes a product comprised in another product, whether as a component part or raw material or otherwise.[68]

Of course a scheme like this means that there may be many defendants. It will often only be necessary for a claimant to identify one legitimate defendant. The rest of the squabbling will be effected by a mass of Part 20 proceedings.

A product has a defect within the meaning of the Act if the safety of the product is not such as persons generally are entitled to expect. This definition was central to the important decision of *A v. National Blood Authority (No.1)*.[69] This was about the infection of a number of claimants with Hepatitis C through blood transfusions. They said that the blood was a defective product; it was not as safe as persons generally were entitled to expect. The defendant, which supplied the blood, said that although it knew that there was a risk of blood products carrying the virus, the

---

64. Which enacted Council Directive (EEC) 85/3274.
65. Section 5.
66. Section 2.
67. Section 4(1)(e).
68. Section 1(2). There is an important caveat in s.1(3), however, a supplier of a product X which comprises other products (Y) is not to be treated simply by reason of his supply of X as a supplier of Y.
69. [2001] 3 All ER 289.

absence of a screening test meant that the risk was unavoidable. This, it contended, entitled it to take refuge in the state of knowledge defence. Knowing the virus was there was one thing, but short of a complete bar on blood products, nothing could be done about it. It would be unfair, they said, to construe the parent Directive so strictly as to impose liability in those circumstances. Not so, held the judge. No 'state of the art' defence was available here. People expected blood to be safe. It was not. That was enough to ground liability.

This is a strict decision. Its effects on the rest of product liability law, particularly in a medical context, have yet to be worked out.

**Limitation**

The law of limitation is legendarily complex and dull. It is also, these days, relatively unimportant. Law, like everything else, has fashions. Limitation was popular 10 years ago. It is now out of fashion.

The basic rule in personal injury cases is that a claim has to be brought within three years of the cause of action accruing (which means the injury occurring),[70] or within three years of the claimant acquiring knowledge of various things – that the injury was "significant"; that the injury was attributable "in whole or in part to the act or omission which is alleged to constitute negligence, nuisance or breach of duty"; and the identity of the defendant.[71] This knowledge includes constructive knowledge, which is: "knowledge which he might reasonably have been expected to acquire (a) from facts ascertainable by him; or (b) from facts

---

70. Limitation Act 1980, s.11.
71. Limitation Act 1980, s.14(1).

ascertainable by him with the help of medical or other appropriate expert advice which it is reasonable for him to seek ..."[72] This section goes on to say that "... a person shall not be fixed ... with knowledge of a fact ascertainable only with the help of expert advice so long as he has taken all reasonable steps to obtain (and, where appropriate, to act on) that advice." A person is at risk of falling foul of limitation, therefore, if he sits wondering about whether he has a claim, instead of getting up and asking solicitors to instruct experts to tell him if he has or not.

This all sounds like stern stuff, and potentially it is. In other areas of law the inflexibility of the limitation rules gives lawyers sleepless nights and fuels a huge parasitic industry of litigation about the financial consequences of missed limitation deadlines. In the medical arena, however, things are cosier for claimants. Section 33 of the Limitation Act 1980 allows the court to disregard the operation of the rules if it is thinks it is equitable to do so. And, increasingly, the court does think it is equitable. In theory, a claimant coming cap in hand to ask for the rigour of the Limitation Act to be mitigated has to show that it is equitable for the limitation period to be disapplied. In practice, the defendant is always on the back foot in such an application, and will have to show that it would be substantially and irremediably prejudiced if the application were successful.

The main reason for the difference between personal injury cases and others is clear: these are the sorts of cases where the claimant is least likely to have the benefit of legal advice at the time of the injury (unlike most other areas of potential claims, which are likely to rest on a transaction which has had some sort of professional legal or quasi-legal input). In clinical negligence cases there will generally be a need for expert medical and legal

---

72. Limitation Act 1980, s.14(3).

advice to distinguish between the consequences of malpractice and the ordinary misfortunes of life. People damaged by doctors are understandably reluctant to put themselves back into the hands of doctors for the necessary assessment.

In many of the really big clinical negligence cases – the brain-damaged baby cases, for instance – limitation is irrelevant. Time does not run against a person under a legal disability. So if a claimant is a patient within the meaning of the Mental Health Act, and incapable of conducting his own affairs, he is perpetually (or for as long as his incapacity persists) immune to limitation. A child does not acquire legal capacity for the purposes of limitation until the age of 18. Accordingly, many clinical negligence claims involving allegations of injury to children will not become statute barred until the claimant's 21st birthday.

## The future of clinical negligence litigation

For years there have been mutterings about no-fault liability schemes. These are fine in principle, but hugely expensive. It has seemed to most commentators that a fault-based scheme is likely to remain. In June 2003, however, the Chief Medical Officer released his long-awaited report on clinical negligence: *Making Amends*. It has something in it to alarm everyone, and worried barristers and solicitors set up discussion groups and checked on the adequacy of their pension provision. At its heart are two notions: first, that the Woolf reforms have failed to deal effectively with clinical negligence litigation in the way that they are generally thought to have dealt with other types of litigation; and second, that this type of litigation is radically different in nature to other types, and requires a wholly new approach.

A lot of it is wool. It says, at great length and with lots of histograms, what we all know: that clinical negligence litigation is expensive, lengthy and psychologically good for no one but clinical negligence lawyers; that an apology and an explanation is all that a lot of claimants are seeking; and that there are some indefensible anomalies (most notably that a claimant injured in a NHS hospital can claim from the NHS defendant the cost of private treatment for the consequences, yet still get that treatment on the NHS and put on the horses the money saved.)

To the audible relief of many it rejects a no-fault based system of compensation; to the audible disappointment of many it thinks that further evolution of the existing law of tort cannot deliver the necessary goods; and to the audible suspicion of most, proposes the establishment of an entirely new system of redress for avoidable harm to patients caused in the course of NHS treatment.

This would be called the NHS Redress Scheme. It would involve the establishment of a national body (a re-vamped and re-named National Health Service Litigation Authority) which would make payments of up to £30,000. Other compensation would be limited to "the notional cost of the episode of care or other amount as appropriate, at the discretion of the local NHS Trust." No cheques would be written until there had been a full investigation of the complaint or claim (which one would hope there was anyway, under the existing procedures), and there would be "development of a package of the remedial care and rehabilitation where required" (which of course the NHS has a statutory duty to provide anyway.)

The Government is obviously concerned to reduce the cost of brain-damaged baby cases. The report therefore proposes that birth-related neurological impairment should come under the umbrella of the Scheme. The £30,000 ceiling would obviously not apply to such cases. Instead, there would be an initial payment for pain, suffering and loss of amenity, capped at £50,000, a managed care package, a monthly payment for the costs of care which could not be provided through such a package (up to £100,000 per annum in the most severe cases), and one-off lump sum payments for home adaptations and equipment at intervals throughout the child's life (of up to £50,000). Tot that lot up and, if you are an NHS accountant, you will smile. If you are a claimant's lawyer, knowing how dismal the publicly funded facilities for brain-injured children generally are in the UK, you will scoff.

There would be no obligation to use the Scheme – patients would still be able to sue – but in practice there would be considerable pressure to do so. Except in cerebral palsy cases, there would be a presumption that a claimant had first applied to the Scheme. That would be likely to mean that cases meeting the financial criteria of the Scheme would be regarded with deep suspicion by any judge who later came to scrutinise them; there would, in effect, already be a finding against such a claimant.

Another concern about this presumption against litigation is that it might amount to a presumption against really thorough investigation. Whatever one says against the clinical negligence industry, it does a very good job at turning over all the stones under which possible forensic nasties might lie. Anyone involved in it knows how a second and a third expert looking at an apparently hopeless case can often result in a new and original idea which transforms the way an action is argued.

The pressure to enter the Scheme might also, because of the financial caps on the Scheme's compensation, turn out to be pressure to settle for an under-value.

The only obvious advantages of the Scheme are that it would be cheaper to engage in than litigation, might operate at lower emotional temperatures, and might produce a payment faster. The traditionalist's (rather good) rejoinder to that is that if clinical negligence is under-Woolfed, Woolf it up a bit more. There are plenty of reasons why the system is the way it is; revolution can sometimes be a fig-leaf covering up legal and historical ignorance.

Many of the other proposals for claims not falling within the Scheme are eminently sensible.

For instance, statute would impose a duty of candour on clinicians and health service managers, requiring them to inform patients about actions resulting in harm, and there would be exemption from disciplinary action for those reporting adverse events or errors (with some obvious exceptions); periodical payments in larger value cases would be encouraged; the absurdity of the NHS providing restorative care itself, while paying the costs of private care, would be stopped; attempts at mediation would be expected; judges handling clinical negligence cases would receive specialist training.

If these proposals, or anything like them, become law, clinical negligence litigation will be a very different business. There will be no time for gladiatorial spats. *Bolam* will remain the law, but law written in a book which is never taken off the shelf. The judges will become the managers of care packages; the lawyers will become ever more indistinguishable from accountants.

# CHAPTER 5

# THE LAW OF DEATH

## Introduction

The English law is slightly more coherent about death than life. There is a fair consensus in the law about what death is, and that it is a bad thing. The law goes to great lengths to prevent it, but is philosophically queasy in the shadowlands between obvious death and obvious life. It is reluctant to concede that the ECHR has anything to add to the traditional wisdom of the common law. When it comes to analysing the status of the body after death, the law is chaotic and behind the times. It investigates deaths fairly thoroughly, mainly to prevent further deaths, and also because it acknowledges the cathartic value to the bereaved of investigation.

## What death is and what death isn't

In their definitions of death, the judges have more or less kept pace with science. When science thought that death was defined by cessation of breathing, the judges thought so too. Doctors have now adopted the brain death criterion of death, and the brain stem criterion of brain death.[1] The brain stem powers the basic functions of heart beat and respiration. Once it is dead, recovery of these functions is inconceivable. Brain stem death necessarily implies death of higher brain function: the converse is not true. A brain stem death criterion of death is therefore, and importantly, more conservative than one based on irretrievable loss of consciousness.

---

1. See, for example, *Re A (A Minor)* [1992] 3 Med LR 303.

Patients in persistent vegetative state are therefore alive - a conclusion which leads to some formidable legal and analytic difficulties which are discussed below.

**Murder and euthanasia**

Murder is killing someone, intending to kill them or intending to cause grievous bodily harm. Intention and motive are completely different. Killing somebody intentionally with the motive of preventing them from suffering continuing pain is still murder. It is very simple; euthanasia is murder, and carries a mandatory life sentence. There is a curious and important doctrine, however, which needs to be understood: the law of double effect.

The principle of double effect has sometimes blurred, in the eyes of laymen, the distinction between intention and motive. The two remain analytically wholly different. The principle says that if one does something to a patient with the intention of (for example) reducing pain, and that action has the undesired but inevitable effect of causing their death, the relevant intention for the purposes of the law of murder is that of pain reduction. Accordingly, the doctor who has administered the fatal dose would not be guilty of murder. This seems like classical legal sophistry, and there is no doubt that it has resulted in some doctors being acquitted, on technically inaccurate grounds, of murder. But nonetheless, when wielded properly, it has the effect, which most people would think is ethically right, of preventing doctors from being speared fatally on one or other horn of a clinical dilemma. Society imposes on doctors a duty to stop pain; it also imposes on them a duty not to kill. Sometimes those duties conflict. It would not be fair to lock doctors up with their own chamber pots simply because they have been caught in the philosophical cross-fire between those two duties.

Lord Joffe has recently attempted to introduce a Bill which would legalise euthanasia. It stands little chance of becoming law, but has provoked a lot of discussion. The promoters of the Bill said that they had learned the lessons taught by the Dutch experience of euthanasia. There is evidence that the Dutch legislation, which permits voluntary euthanasia (when the patient freely requests euthanasia) is being abused by clinicians, and that clinicians are making their own decisions about when patients should die. The Joffe Bill has an elaborate system which is designed to ensure that this could not happen, and also that decisions about euthanasia would be made entirely freely, after a full explanation of all the clinical facts, including the availability and likely efficacy of palliative care. If this Bill became law, some interesting legal arguments would arise. Palliative care physicians are almost to a man against euthanasia, on the grounds that there is no pain which cannot, with competent care, be controlled. If they are right, the law would require doctors to tell their patients this, and (a) no sane person would then consent to euthanasia; and (b) even if they did so consent, since there would be no sufficient clinical indication, it would presumably be unlawful for the doctor to perform the act. It may therefore be that all the fuss which the Bill has generated might be stilled by a determination simply of the truth or otherwise of the palliativists' claim. If the Bill became law, it would presumably be possible for a doctor to commit murder or manslaughter by obtaining the patient's consent to euthanasia, having failed (deliberately or negligently) to tell him the full story about the palliative options. If a doctor deliberately withheld information in the knowledge that, without the appropriate reassurance about the efficacy of palliative care, the patient would ask for euthanasia, there would be sufficient intention to kill to ground a charge of murder, and yet this would be a true omission – classically regarded as inadequate for murder.

## The geography of rocks and hard places: the Siamese Twins' Case[2]

All this is relatively straightforward. But medicine has a habit of confounding neat analytic categories. The most dramatic recent example was the case of the conjoined twins. The considerations of the Court of Appeal dealt very directly with what the court thought about what human life really consisted in and whether human lives could be weighed against one another. It has potentially explosive significance for the law of medical murder.

### *Introduction*

Jodie and Mary were Siamese twins. They shared a common aorta. Mary relied on Jodie's heart to keep her alive. Without Jodie, Mary would probably have died *in utero*. Even with Jodie, Mary could not live for long. The burden of pumping blood for Mary as well as herself put a terrible burden on Jodie's heart. If Jodie was not separated from Mary, Jodie would herself die soon. But the twins could be surgically separated. That surgical separation would take away Mary's blood supply. She would die. But it would enable Jodie to live a relatively normal life.

The hospital wanted to separate the twins. The parents refused to give their consent to the separation. So the issue came before the court. Johnson J decided that the separation could occur. The parents appealed. The Court of Appeal (Ward, Brooke and Robert Walker LJJ) unanimously decided that the separation could go ahead.

---

2.  *Re A (Conjoined Twins: Medical Treatment)* [2001] Fam 147.

## The basic approach

All three judges agreed on how to approach the question of whether the surgery should be carried out. There are two broad stages. The first is a family law stage, decided by reference to the usual question: where does the best interests of each child lie? Since there are two children here, if their interests lie in wholly incompatible places, how are the competing claims resolved? The second stage is a criminal law stage. If the family law considerations decree that the operation can be performed, is it otherwise lawful to perform it?

## The family law questions

There were three crucial questions. First, is it in Jodie's best interests to be separated from Mary? Second, is it in Mary's best interests to be separated from Jodie? Third, if the answer to either of these first two questions is no, how can the court resolve the conflicting interests?

Each of the judges started from the premise (which had been questioned by some commentators interviewed by the media) that Mary and Jodie were independent human beings with legal rights, including a right to life.

None of the judges had any difficulty concluding that it was in Jodie's best interest to be separated from Mary. The medical evidence about this was overwhelming.

Ward and Brooke LJJ decided that it was not in Mary's best interests to be separated from Jodie. If she were not separated from Jodie, Mary would have a pitiable few months, and then die. There was no reliable way to assess whether she was in pain. She might be, but this, said the two judges, was not the important question. What was important was whether her life during those few months was worth nothing. Both judges found that, although that life was lived in terrible circumstances, it still had value and dignity. It could not be said to be in Mary's interest to take that life away.

Importantly, they distinguished between Mary's situation and the situation facing doctors who withdraw life-sustaining treatment on the grounds that to continue to receive it is not in the best interests of the patient. The distinction was simply based on the observation that Mary was receiving no life-sustaining treatment at all. The surgery was not withdrawing something which the doctors had started.

Robert Walker LJ, in a chilling judgment, disagreed. He said that since Mary's continued life held nothing but possible pain and discomfort, if indeed she can feel anything at all, it was in her best interests to do the operation which would end her life. Curiously he relied, in coming to this conclusion, on the notion that an intrinsic part of the right to life is a right to bodily integrity and autonomy. The purpose of the operation would not be to kill Mary, but, *inter alia*, to give Mary as well as Jodie, the bodily integrity and autonomy which nature had denied them.

He therefore saw no conflict between the interests of Jodie and Mary.

But Ward and Brooke LJJ, having decided that there was a clear conflict between the interests of Jodie and Mary, had to go further and decide how the conflict could be resolved. They toyed with the idea of saying that the question was too difficult for any court, but eventually decided that they could not duck it. The welfare of one child had to be balanced against the other. The right of each to life was of course equal. It was not legitimate to value the quality of one life as greater or lesser than any other. But it was relevant to consider what the performance and the non-performance of the treatment would mean for each child. Mary was, and had always been, "*fated for early death.*" Jodie was salvageable. Accordingly, balancing the competing interests, the balance lay in favour of giving Jodie the chance of life which only surgery could give her.

## The criminal law questions

Having decided that, so far as the family law considerations were concerned, the operation should go ahead, the court still had to satisfy itself that the operation was lawful. The hurdle was, of course, the law of murder.

Brooke LJ's analysis was the one which will interest criminal lawyers most. In all but his conclusion about the relevance of necessity, it was wholly conventional. In his summary he said that four issues arose:

> *"Is Mary a human being in the eyes of the law? The answer is yes. Would the proposed operation amount to the positive act of killing Mary? The answer is yes. Would the doctors be held to have the intention of killing Mary, however little they desire that outcome? The answer is again yes. The doctrine of double effect, which permits a doctor, acting in good faith, to administer pain-killing drugs to her dying patient, has no relevance in this case. This leaves open the single question? Would the killing be unlawful?"*

He did not consider at any length the self-defence/defence of others approach of Ward LJ, but probably regarded those ideas as inherent in the doctrine of necessity, which he dealt with in great detail. Most lawyers will remember the case of *Dudley v. Stephens*,[3] where survivors of a shipwreck, at sea in an open boat, killed and ate the cabin boy. At their trials for murder, they pleaded necessity, saying that if they had not killed the boy they would themselves

---

3. (1884) 14 QBD 273.

have died. It was held that that plea was not open to them. That decision was affirmed by the House of Lords in 1987, in *R. v. Howe*.[4]

These authorities would obviously be a significant obstacle in the way of any advocate representing any surgeon who killed Mary by cutting off her blood supply so that Jodie could live. Brooke LJ, however, decided that the policy objections to the doctrine of necessity which underlay the authorities did not apply to the very special circumstances of this case.

The first policy objection was the impossibility of judging objectively the comparative value of lives. But this was an objection which had already been answered in this case when deciding the family law question about the competing interests of Mary and Jodie. Mary was bound to die anyway. Jodie was not.

The second policy objection was that a defence of necessity would divide law wholly from morality. But there was far from a moral consensus that it would be wrong to separate the twins. There were competing, valid ethical views, and the court should not choose between them. *"All that a court can say,"* said Brooke LJ *"is that it is not at all obvious that this is the sort of clear-cut situation, leading to a divorce of law from morality, which was of such concern to our predecessors in 1884."* This is difficult to follow. Almost by definition every case in which necessity might be invoked is ethically ambiguous. There must have been a tremendous moral debate in that lifeboat.

Accordingly, since the policy considerations underlying the rejection of the defence of necessity did not apply here, the defence could be raised in this case.

Although he said that he agreed with Brooke LJ on the criminal law questions, Ward LJ's analysis was rather different. He

---

4. [1987] 1 AC 417.

had two main points. The first arose from noting that the law imposes on doctors a duty to do what is best for their patients. In the case of the twins the imposition of that duty creates exactly the same conflict which faced the court when considering the family law questions. The doctors are under a duty to operate because that is in Jodie's best interests, and under a duty not to operate because not to operate is in Mary's best interests. Since the law itself creates that conflict, said Ward LJ, the law must allow it to be resolved by making it possible for doctors to choose the lesser of two evils without being guilty of murder. This comes very close to saying (as Robert Walker LJ did explicitly), that the *bona fide* exercise of clinical judgment which will have the inevitable result of a death cannot co-exist with the *mens rea* of murder.

Second, he noted that there is no absolute rule that killing a human being, intending to kill him or her, amounts to murder. Killing in those circumstances in self-defence or the defence of others would be no crime. The "aggression" which necessitates the self-defence or the defence of others need not be unlawful for the defence to be made out. He gave the example of killing a six-year-old boy who was shooting others indiscriminately in a playground. The six-year-old would be too young for his actions to be classified as unlawful, and yet to kill in self-defence or the defence of others would not be murder. Ward LJ saw no difference in principle between that case and the case of doctors who killed Mary in order to stop her killing Jodie.

Robert Walker LJ appeared to suggest that the doctrine of double effect would give the surgeons a defence to a charge of murder, and further (relying on *Gillick v. West Norfolk and Wisbech AHA*[5]), that at least in the circumstances of this case, where a doctor exercises clinical judgment in a *bona fide* way the

---

5. [1986] AC 112.

exercise would be wholly incompatible with the *mens rea* of murder. He also thought that the defence of necessity would apply, and that if it were necessary to extend the existing common law doctrine of necessity to cover these circumstances, then it should be extended. In common with the other judges, he found that the Human Rights Act gave little help.

## Where this leaves the law

The Court of Appeal emphasised repeatedly the highly unusual circumstances of this case. But, nonetheless, making all allowances for the oddness of the facts, this case is highly legally significant.

The court has shown itself prepared to weigh one life against another. Although Ward and Brooke LJJ tried hard to avoid language which suggested that the value of a human life consisted in an outside observer's assessment of the worthwhileness and the likely duration of the life, there is no escaping the fact that two short, frustrating and possibly painful lives have been found in a fundamental way to be worth less than one relatively normal, relatively long life.

Robert Walker LJ was scarily clear: a short, terribly disabled and possibly painful life was a life not worth living. Mary was better off dead than alive.

Ward and Brooke LJ's judgments on the family law issues are likely to be preferred. If they are, the family law questions inherent in most medical cases remain more or less unchanged, and a workable framework for resolving competing interests has been laid down. Robert Walker LJ's view, if followed, leads logically straight to judicially endorsed euthanasia.

The case has thrown a number of elements of the criminal law into doubt. Most of us, including the House of Lords, evidently thought that *Dudley v. Stephens* said that there was no defence of necessity to murder. If it is not as simple as that, then the House of

Lords ought soon to tell us why.

The existing boundaries of the doctrine of double effect have been challenged. Ward and Brooke LJJ's understanding of the doctrine is the conventional one, but if it really does have the wider scope which Robert Walker LJ implied that it might have, this needs to be determined.

Robert Walker LJ, and less obviously Ward LJ, have raised the possibility that professional judgment, exercised *bona fide*, is incompatible with criminal intent. If that is so then medical "murder" simply does not fit the mould of ordinary murder.

## Medical manslaughter

Manslaughter, in a medical context, is killing by gross negligence.[6] It is increasingly common for doctors to find themselves in the dock, facing conviction and imprisonment.[7] The public seems to want or need the cathartic experience of such prosecutions. Typical examples of acts and omissions which have been found to be sufficiently negligent are where an anaesthetist wanders off in the middle of an operation, leaving his entirely dependent patient dangerously vulnerable, or where a doctor mistakenly injects a cytotoxic drug into the spinal cord of a patient.

The negligence, to qualify as gross negligence, must be negligence which is dramatically outside the generous penumbra of *Bolam*-acceptability, and the overall conduct must be such as to warrant the extreme censure of society which criminal conviction

---

6. See *R. v. Adomako* [1995] 1 AC 171.
7. For a discussion of several recent cases see: The criminalisation of fatal medical mistakes: BMJ 2003; 327:1118-9 (Editorial).

entails.[8]

This sounds odd. It is circular. It amounts to saying: In order to find the defendant guilty of the crime you must find that he is guilty of a crime. Criticism of this circularity was at the heart of the appeal in *R. v. Misra and Srivastava*.[9] The two defendants were doctors. They had failed to appreciate that a patient was as ill as he was. In fact he had toxic shock syndrome. He did not get the treatment he should have had, and he died. The jury convicted both defendants of gross negligence manslaughter.

Both defendants appealed, translating into legal language the vague disquiet about the circularity of the definition of "gross negligence". Article 7 of the ECHR, they said, supported their contention that there is a principle of "legal certainty", and that any criminal offence which is insufficiently certain will not be Article 7 (or Article 6) compliant. Article 7 prohibits the creation of criminal offences which have retrospective application.

The Court of Appeal had no difficulty in concluding that Article 7 was indeed an example of such a principle. But it was not the architect. Bacon, in the seventeenth century, had made things far clearer than Article 7 did: "... if the trumpet gives an uncertain sound, who shall prepare himself to the battle? So if the law gives an uncertain sound, who shall prepare to obey it? It ought therefore to warn before it strikes ..." There is abundant subsequent authority, on both sides of the Atlantic, for the principle.[10] The

---

8. See *R. v. Bateman* (1925) 19 Cr.App. R 8: "*In order to establish criminal liability, the facts must be such that ... the negligence of the accused went beyond a mere matter of compensation between subjects and showed such disregard for the life and safety of others as to amount to a crime against the State and conduct deserving punishment.*" Per Lord Hewart CJ at 11.
9. [2004] EWCA Crim. 2375.
10. See, for example, *SW v. UK* [1995] 21 EHRR 363; *Grayned v. City of Rockford*, 408 US 104; *Fothergill v. Monarch Airlines Ltd.* [1981] AC 251; *Warner v. Commissioner of Police for the Metropolis* [1969] 2 AC 256.

ECHR added little or nothing, but it was a salutary reminder of the old common law idea.

The requirement is not for absolute, but for sufficient certainty. The court adopted the judgment in *Sunday Times v. UK*.[11] The law must be formulated:

> "... *with sufficient precision to enable the citizen to regulate his conduct: he must be able – if need be with appropriate advice – to foresee to a degree that is reasonable in the circumstances, the consequences which any given action may entail. Those consequences need not be foreseeable with absolute certainty: experience shows this to be unobtainable. Again, whilst certainty is highly desirable, it may bring in its train excessive rigidity, and the law must be able to keep pace with changing circumstances. Accordingly, many laws are inevitably couched in terms which, to a greater or lesser extent, are vague, and whose interpretation and application are questions of practice.*"

The court said that gross negligence manslaughter did not breach the principle. That was what the House of Lords had said in *Adomako*, and the fact that the old *Adomako* submissions could now be framed in the language of Strasbourg did not make them more persuasive. There was no real circularity, but if there was, it was not dangerous.

> "*On proper analysis ... the jury is not deciding whether the particular defendant ought to be convicted on some unprincipled basis. The question for the jury is not whether the defendant's negligence was gross, and whether, <u>additionally</u>,*

---

11. [1979] 2 EHRR 245.

*it was a crime, but whether his behaviour was grossly negligent and <u>consequently</u> criminal. This is not a question of law, but one of fact, for decision in the individual case."* (Original emphasis).

Reference in the direction to the jury to the criminal law was useful. It avoided the danger that the jury might equate "simple" negligence (which in the context of a manslaughter allegation would not be a crime at all) with negligence which involves a criminal offence.

Relying on the dictum of Lord Bingham in *R. v. G*,[12] the defendants contended that, with the exception of causing death by dangerous driving, no serious criminal offence could be committed without *mens rea*. Gross negligence manslaughter should, they said be replaced by reckless manslaughter.

This was given short shrift, on the ground that Lord Bingham had emphasised that he was not considering any context other than the Criminal Damage Act 1971. But even if a mental element was necessary, the requirement of fault or culpability satisfied the requirement:

> "As a matter of strict language, "mens rea" is ... used to describe the ingredient of fault or culpability required before criminal liability for the defendant's actions may be established. In Sweet v. Parsley [1970] AC 132, Lord Reid explained that there were occasions when gross negligence provided the 'necessary mental element' for a serious crime. Manslaughter by gross negligence is not an absolute offence. The requirement for gross negligence provides the necessary element of culpability."

---

12. [2004] 1 AC 1034.

There has been considerable academic discussion of the nature of the risk which, in a true case of gross negligence manslaughter, a reasonably prudent person would have foreseen. Is it a risk of death? Or of serious injury? *Adomako* says that it is the risk of death. *R. v. Bateman*,[13] referred unhelpfully to "disregard of the life and safety of others." The court has hopefully silenced the discussion.

> *"In our judgment, where the issue of risk is engaged, Adomako demonstrated, and it is now clearly established, that it relates to the risk of death, and is not sufficiently satisfied by the risk of bodily injury or injury to health ..."*

*Misra* will not satisfy everyone. Those intuitive concerns about circularity will survive the careful reasoning of the Court of Appeal. The judgment failed to deal with a crucial practical point – how the grossness of the negligence is established. It is done by calling expert witnesses: the prosecution witness says that the negligence is gross: the defence witness says that it is not. How can a lay jury possibly decide on any rational basis who is right? Too often the good character, and possibly liberty, of doctors and other professionals depends simply on an expert witness beauty parade. However nicely that is wrapped up jurisprudentially, it remains offensive.

## Switching off: (1) the strange case of *Bland*

There are some cases which force judges to become philosophers and theologians. The best examples are those cases which involve patients who hover outside the normal human community; beyond

---

13.   19 Cr.App. R 8.

the usual analytic categories; neither quite alive nor quite dead. The classic case is that of Tony Bland.[14]

Tony Bland was a young victim of the Hillsborough Disaster. He lay for years in a persistent vegetative state (PVS). His cerebral cortex was effectively destroyed. He could breathe spontaneously, but needed to be artificially fed and hydrated. The medical evidence was that he could feel no pain, no pleasure, or experience anything at all. He could not communicate in any way. Indeed there was nothing going on in his brain which could be communicated. The prognosis was hopeless: he would never get any better. His family and the treating clinicians agreed that the artificial feeding and nutrition which were keeping him alive should be stopped. But there was a problem. They would be doing something which would obviously have the intention of ending his life. It would end his life. Why was that not murder? The case went to the House of Lords.

The most important thing to remember about the House of Lords decision in *Bland* is the House's agenda. It needed to ensure that the doctors were not guilty of murder. That result was unthinkable. Other principles became servants of this aim.

Because there were five judges and five speeches, there was no one route to the decision. But there were some common threads in the reasoning. The important elements of the decision were as follows:

(a) *Tony Bland was alive*

This was not an inevitable conclusion. Human life could have been defined in terms of ability to enjoy life; to experience; to relate; or otherwise in terms of cortical brain function.[15] But

---

14. *Airedale NHS Trust v. Bland* [1993] AC 789.
15. The families of PVS victims often say that the victim is not really alive: that their body is still there but that which made the person human has fled.

the brain stem death definition of death was adopted. This was necessary to prevent some toxic philosophical fall-out in areas far away from *Bland*, but it meant that the possibility of murder still had to be dealt with.

(b) *Human life was sacred*
All of the judges said this. Each seems to have meant something rather different by it. If one looks at the ways in which judges in the various common law jurisdictions have considered the sanctity of human life in the context of PVS cases, four views emerge: (1) That biological human life is sacred. (2) That what is sacred is the bundle of human characteristics which, if possessed, allows a being to be described as human. (3) That what are sacred are the rights which the law says that a human possesses. (4) That what is sacred is the human's status as a member of the human community – with the implication that inability to participate in that community means loss of the status. There are obvious circularities in these definitions.

The House of Lords seems to have adopted, although rather equivocally, view (2). Although the House expressly said that Tony Bland was still alive and still human because his brain stem worked, it appears to have said that that life need not be preserved because the sanctity which once attached to it had consisted in, and evaporated with the departure of, his ability to experience and to relate.

(c) *The artificial feeding and hydration amounted to medical treatment*
This was fair enough. It required sophisticated medical and nursing care. It was not like feeding a baby with a spoon. Tony Bland could not co-operate in any way with his own feeding or hydration.

(d) *Stopping treatment would be an omission, not an act*
This was at the heart of the decision, as will become clear. Its importance is worrying for people who think that the law is built on a secure analytic edifice. There are two reasons for this. First, as demonstrated by the example of the trolley problem, which is discussed below, there are real philosophical reasons to doubt the reality, let alone the utility, of the distinction between acts and omission. And second, any half-competent advocate can turn an act into an omission and back again. This is not necessarily for the reasons which lie at the basis of the genuine philosophical objections, although the better class of barrister might draw on those ideas. Generally it will be done by way of semantic tricks played with the facts. In the case of the cessation of artificial feeding, food which was previously given will not be given. That looks like an omission to feed. But the feeding tube will be withdrawn; that looks like an act. An order will have been given; do not feed. That looks like an act. And so on.

(e) *Doctors have a duty to act in the patient's best interests*
This is trite law. It can be put more forcibly. Doctors are only entitled to do anything at all to a patient insofar as it is in the patient's best interests; anything else will be an unlawful invasion for which the doctor can be liable in damages.

The judges considered long, hard and theologically the isolated issue of where Tony Bland's best interests lay. Those deliberations are discussed below. But because the broader question related to the doctors' duty to act in the best interests of the patient, the *Bolam* test was applied to determine whether "best interests" had been determined in a responsible way.

This is strange and controversial. It makes otiose the deeper philosophical considerations about "best interests" which the judges were anxious to say lay at the root of their conclusions. It introduces a real element of subjectivity into life and death decision-making. In a human rights context, how can one say meaningfully that there is an absolute right to life if, as a matter of fact, life can be lawfully taken where a mere body of responsible clinicians agrees to it being taken? The *Bolam* test is no defence to murder; why should it be a defence to an allegation that life has been otherwise unlawfully taken?

To use the *Bolam* test in these circumstances is really to set up a great game of conceptual pass-the-parcel. The doctors are told by the courts to come to court so that the courts can decide whether the best interests of the patient lie in the continuation or the withdrawal of treatment. And the courts then answer the question by deferring to the doctors. The doctors are entitled to be subjective in making their decision about best interests, according to the courts, but the courts insist on rubber-stamping the subjective decision by reference to other subjective decisions from experts. There is a dizzying circularity about all this. Nowhere in the cycle is anyone forced to confront the fundamental, absolute question: is it better for a PVS patient to be brain stem alive or brain stem dead?

For the court to deploy the *Bolam* test is ultimately to abdicate responsibility for uncomfortable and technically tricky decision-making.

Further consideration of the intellectual probity of the *Bolam* test in these circumstances appears below, in the section on human rights issues.

(e) *Tony Bland had no interests*
Assuming the prognosis was correct, it could not be said, thought the judges, that he had any personal interests at all. Note that this assumes a lot about what the essence of a human is, as has been pointed out at para. (b) above. "Having an interest" appears to have been construed as "Having an interest and being able to appreciate that you have that interest". This is a gloss frowned on by conservative commentators. They think that human worth is intrinsic and does not consist in the ability to do or to experience, and accordingly does not vanish when those faculties leave.

Medical decisions about "best interests" are, of course, the results of balancing exercises. Doctors balance the interests in starting or continuing treatment against the interests in not starting or stopping it. It is not easy to see what interest Tony Bland had in the withdrawal of treatment. It necessarily meant that he died. It could be said that, had he been conscious of it, he would not have wanted to survive in the pitiful state of dependence which is PVS. The answer to that is that he was not conscious of it – a fact which compelled Butler-Sloss in a later PVS case to conclude that PVS patients have no Article 3 rights at all. If Tony Bland had no interests at all, there was nothing to weigh in the balancing exercise; that exercise was simply meaningless. The logical thing to do in those circumstances is to maintain the *status quo*. Determining the *status quo* is not as easy as it sounds. It is not necessarily just continuing the feeding. *Absent* positive intervention (which, with the benefit of hindsight, was utterly pointless), the *status quo* would have been death.

Interests and rights are not the same. The House heard the case long before the ECHR was grafted into the English law. The impact of the ECHR on PVS cases is considered below. It is enough to say at this stage that the courts have subsequently behaved as if interests and rights are indistinguishable, and that a PVS patient has neither.

(f) *Because Tony Bland had no interest in staying alive, there was no duty to keep him alive*
Indeed, this can be put more strongly. Since doctors can only intervene when it is in the patient's best interests to do so, to continue the positive intervention of feeding and hydration would be unlawful.

If this is right, it would be unfair to lock a doctor up under the law of murder because he refused to do something which the law of assault said he was not allowed to do. The next and final step was to work out how to avoid a conviction of murder.

(g) *This was not murder because: (i) withdrawal of feeding was an omission, not an act; and (ii) (possibly), medical judgment exercised bona fide was inconsistent with the mens rea of murder*
Reason (ii) is a fudge. It is answering the problem "Why is this not murder?" by saying: "Because it isn't", or at least, "Because it shouldn't be". Some of the difficulties associated with it are mentioned at (e) above. Its intellectual disreputability has been generally recognised, and subsequent judges have been coy about using it. It was not, for instance, regarded as a get-out-of-jurisprudential jail card in the Conjoined Twins case, although it was suggested by one of the judges there as a solution.

Reason (i) needs a closer look. It is a long-standing principle of English criminal law that an act is necessary for murder. No lay person is under a duty to save anyone from death, and accordingly no lay person can be subject to any criminal sanction for any omission to act to save. A doctor is under a duty to save from death in some circumstances, but where he considers that it would not be in the patient's best interests to intervene to save, and that decision is endorsed by a responsible body of medical opinion, he can be subject to no criminal sanction for his failure to save. Acts are different. It was not in dispute that either a lay person or a doctor would have been guilty of murder had they committed the act of pressing the plunger of a syringe which injected potassium chloride heart-stoppingly into Tony Bland's circulation. The results in these cases seem to make ethical sense. But it is not necessarily so. In the section on euthanasia, above, a case is posited where a deliberate, malicious killing might result from a failure to give information – as clear an example of an omission as one can find.

Consider the following example. It is called the "Trolley Problem".

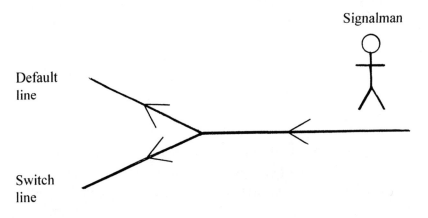

Imagine that you are a signalman. By pulling a lever (which is certainly an act), you can divert a train from the "default line" (to which it will go if you do nothing), onto the "switch line." Imagine, in each example, that you know very well that any person on either the default line or the switch line will be killed if the train goes down that line. Now consider the following examples:

(a) You see a man standing on the switch line. You pull the lever. He is killed.
(b) You see a man standing on the default line. You do not pull the lever. He is killed.
(c) You see 100 men standing on the default line. One of them is your enemy. There is no one on the switch line. You do not pull the lever. All the men on the default line are killed.
(d) You see two men standing on the default line and one man on the switch line. Thinking that it is better to save two by sacrificing one, you pull the lever. The man on the switch line is killed.
(e) You see one man standing on the default line and two men on the switch line. The man on the default line is your brother. To save him you pull the lever. The two men on the switch line are killed.
(f) You see two men standing on the default line and one man on the switch line. The man on the switch line is your enemy. You pull the lever and he is killed.
(g) You see one man standing on the default line and two men on the switch line. One of the men on the switch line is your enemy. You pull the lever and both men on the switch line are killed.

In (a) there is no legal difficulty. You are guilty of murder. In (b), there is a culpable omission to act, which might well, since signalmen are under a duty to make safe decisions, make you guilty of manslaughter. But there is no act, and therefore no murder. The answer should be the same for (c). But in (d) a good motive results in a lethal act accompanied by an intention to kill. The doctrine of double effect cannot help here, because different people are involved; there is no benefit at all to the people killed. On the law as it stands, there would be the real possibility of a murder conviction. The likely outcomes in the remaining examples can be worked out from this.

All this points up the fact that the act/omission distinction, which is designed to produce ethically agreeable results, can produce precisely the opposite. *Bland's* reliance on the distinction, although it produced in the case of *Bland* itself a result with which most people would agree, has the potential to wreak real destruction in other cases.

## Switching off (2): less extreme cases

In the case of unconscious or incompetent patients, the position is as it was for Tony Bland. The clinicians can only continue to maintain the patient if they consider it is in the patient's best interests.

Where the patient is conscious, and asks for the support to be withdrawn, the only question is whether he is competent to make the decision. Obviously the level of understanding of the consequences of withdrawing treatment will, since withdrawal is final, have to be very high, and a correspondingly high degree of mental competence will be demanded. But where an appropriate degree of competence is established, continued support against the patient's will will be an assault. The clinicians are not only entitled to withdraw support: they must.

## Human rights considerations in the case of unconscious patients

One would have thought that the ECHR would have had something to say about all this. But the English courts do not think it does.

The issue of the relevance of Articles 2, 3 and 8 to PVS patients arose in *NHS Trust A v M*.[16] This was only a first instance decision, but it was a decision of the President of the Family Division, Dame Butler-Sloss, who bestrides the world of PVS like a colossus.

She was in no doubt that PVS patients were alive, and agreed that the intention of the withdrawal of treatment was to bring about death. But it did not follow from this, she said, that a withdrawal decision which was in the patient's best interests was intentional deprivation of life within the meaning of Article 2. Deprivation of life in that sense meant a deliberate act (not an omission). An omission to provide treatment might amount to a breach of Article 2 where there was a positive obligation to prolong life, but there was no such obligation here. How did one decide whether there was such an obligation? By using the *Bolam* test, of course. If a responsible body of medical opinion said that it was in the patient's best interests to discontinue treatment, then there could be no positive obligation to prolong life, and hence no Article 2 breach.

This conclusion on Article 2 was effectively determinative of the Article 3 and 8 issues. Whatever those Articles said, they could not contradict what Article 2 had decreed. Article 8 was primarily useful as an aid to the construction of Article 2; it helped to determine the scope of the Article 2 obligation.

Article 3 was less craven. It could not merely help Article 2 to its conclusion, so it had to be dismissed. This was done by saying

---

16. [2001] 2 WLR 942.

simply that it did not apply because in order to be degraded or undergo inhumane treatment within the meaning of Article 3, one had to be aware of the degradation or the inhumane treatment.

There are many objections to these conclusions. Some of them have been mentioned above in the consideration of the use of the *Bolam* test to determine best interests. In the human rights context those objections look even stronger. Article 2 gives an absolute right to life. There is nothing absolute about *Bolam*. By its very nature it is a relative test, acknowledging the possibility that there will be differing views about medical matters. But if the medical matters in issue are determinative of life and death, and there is an absolute right to life, one needs an absolute test. Dilute Article 2 with *Bolam*, and Article 2's nature changes: it no longer gives the absolute protection which it says it does: it no longer enshrines the high view of the sanctity of human life which the judges say they hold.

While it is understandable that Butler-Sloss P would not want to come to a conclusion on Article 8 which contradicted Article 2, to say that Article 8 is only useful here as an aid to the construction of Article 2 is curious. The Articles are free-standing. It is commonplace for judges to find that one Article is engaged and another is not. One can see, if not agree with, the notion that Article 8 rights have to be capable of being experienced to be protected by the courts, but although that was the way that the President dealt with Article 3, it was not the way she dealt with Article 8. On its face, even if Article 2 is legitimately side-stepped by the use of the *Bolam* test, to cause someone's death does interfere pretty significantly with their ability to enjoy a private or family life. Again, the objection that no enjoyment would in any event have been possible because a cerebral cortex was necessary for such enjoyment was not relied upon here.

Article 8 would be a useful vehicle for determining the court's attitude towards the relevance of resources. Article 8(2) excuses what would otherwise be a breach of Article 8 on a number of grounds, including public safety, the protection of health, and the protection of the rights and freedoms of others. If Article 8(1) is engaged in the case of a PVS patient, it would seem at least arguable that Article 8(2) would prevent there being a breach, on the grounds that to continue to maintain the patient will necessarily mean, NHS resources being finite, that other patients will be deprived of those resources, and suffer. It could further be said with a straight face that the emotional and physical drainage caused to the carers of PVS patients brought the 8(2) excuses into play. In *Bland* the House of Lords pointedly refused to consider the question of the relevance of resources.

It is not just the Article 8 rights of the patient which need to be considered. Both the continued existence and the death of the patient potentially affect the family and other carers. Even if the patient is incapable of enjoying the fruits of a relationship with others, those others are capable of enjoying a relationship with the patient. The President, without finally deciding the point, doubted whether anyone else's Article 8 rights were engaged. This, again, is strange, particularly since Article 8 apparently does not help the patient. If one is going to deny patients' rights on the grounds, broadly, that they are unconscious, there seems a stronger, not a weaker case for granting Article 8 rights to those carers who, by reason of a patient's unconsciousness, have to shoulder more responsibility for the patient, identify more closely with the patient, and enter into a deeper and more troubling relationship with the patient.

The President's conclusion on Article 3 has been much questioned. If PVS patients are alive and human, then surely the most basic belief in human dignity necessitates the conclusion that, even if the person cannot know how they are being degraded, they retain a right not to be degraded. In the *Leslie Burke* case Munby J, in a very powerful judgment, dissented from the President's conclusion about the relevance of Article 3 to insensate patients. He said:

> *"... I agree that, however unconscious or unaware of ill-treatment a particular incompetent adult or a baby may be, treatment which has the effect on those who witness it of degrading the individual may come within Article 3. Otherwise ... the Convention's emphasis on the protection of the vulnerable may be circumvented."*[17]

But until an appellate court gets a chance to reconsider these issues, it appears to be the case that the ECHR has effectively nothing to say about the position of PVS patients – arguably the most vulnerable patients and, therefore, those most in need of the Convention's protection.

## Can doctors be forced to keep a patient alive?

In the case of an unconscious patient this question turns on where the best interests of the patient is deemed to lie. In the case of a conscious patient, no-one, apart, evidently, from Leslie Burke, doubted that there was an obligation on the NHS (although not, of course, on the individual clinicians concerned), to take reasonable steps to keep the patient alive if he wants to be kept alive.

Leslie Burke suffers from a condition similar to multiple sclerosis. In future he will need artificial nutrition and hydration

---

17. *R. v. General Medical Council, ex parte Burke* [2004] EWHC 1879 at para. 145 – a conclusion supported, *inter alia,* by reference to *D v. UK* (1997) 24 EHRR 423; *Keenan v. UK* (2001) 33 EHRR 913 and *R. Wilkinson v. Broadmoor Special Hospital Authority* [2002] 1 WLR 419.

(ANH) in order to survive. At the time that he needs it he is likely to be competent. The GMC's guidelines on ANH focus on the right of competent patients to refuse treatment. They say nothing about the right of competent patients to require treatment. Leslie Burke read them as implying that doctors are entitled to make a decision to withdraw ANH if they consider that withdrawal is in the patient's best interests. He was frightened by this, and, supported vocally by the pro-life lobby, sought judicial review of the guidelines. He wanted a reassurance that if he wanted to be kept alive by ANH, he would be. He got that reassurance, but the way in which he got it was profoundly damaging to the anti-euthanasia cause.

Munby J pointed out that once a patient is admitted into an NHS hospital a duty arises to provide (and to keep on providing) treatment. There is nothing new about this. It has already been discussed in Chapter 4. Of course, it is true that an individual doctor cannot be compelled to provide a particular treatment. That is crucial in maintaining the independent professionalism of doctors. One cannot, for instance, get a mandatory injunction forcing an individual doctor to administer ANH. But that does not mean that the NHS cannot be forced to do it. The inevitable corollary is that an individual doctor who, for whatever reason, will not provide the treatment which should be provided (for which see below), is under a duty to find a doctor who can.

As noted above, in the case of an incompetent patient the answer to this question is easy. The treatment which must be provided is the treatment which is in the patient's "best interests". If the patient's wishes are known (eg by reference to an advanced directive which applies to the precise circumstances which pertain), they will be determinative. In the absence of any information about the patient's own wishes (or in the presence of information about those wishes which falls short of being determinative of the issue), a wider enquiry as to where the best interests lie will have to be carried out. "Best interests" is wider than medical best interests: this again is trite law.

Where the patient is competent the basic question is the same: the treatment which must be provided is that which is in the patient's best interests. The twist is that the patient is the ultimate arbiter of what amounts to his best interests. He is entitled to reject or, subject to the above caveat, demand, treatment for reasons which his doctors may think are objectively stupid and wholly contrary to his best interests.

This is old common law. The same result can be reached by deploying Articles 3 and 8 of the ECHR. The worry for the pro-life lobby in inviting such deployment is that it invites a hymn to autonomy, and autonomy has a nasty tendency to spill out from where it is helpful to where it is not. Here is verse one of the hymn which Munby J sang:

> "*Personal autonomy – the right of self-determination – and dignity are fundamental rights, recognised by the common law and protected by Articles 3 and 8 of the Convention ... The personal autonomy which is protected by Article 8 embraces such matters as how one chooses to pass the closing days and moments of one's life and how one manages one's death ... The dignity interests protected by the Convention include, under Article 8, the preservation of mental stability and, under Article 3, the right to die with dignity and the right to be protected from treatment, or from a lack of treatment, which will result in one dying in avoidably distressing circumstances ... Important as the sanctity of life is, it has to take second place to personal autonomy; and it may have to take second place to human dignity ...*"

That passage is the single greatest judicial gift the Voluntary

Euthanasia Society has had in the UK.

The pro-life lobby has pretended that there was some sort of victory in Munby J's observation that there should, in assessing the best interests of incompetent patients, be a strong presumption in favour of the preservation of life. But that again has long been uncontroversial. Lord Donaldson in *Re J (A Minor) (Wardship: Medical Treatment)*: "*There is without doubt a very strong presumption in favour of a course of action which will prolong life ...*"[18] In *Bland*, Lord Goff said: "*Of course, in the great majority of cases, the best interests of the patient are likely to require that [life-sustaining] treatment ... if available, should be given to a patient ...*"[19]

## The use of bodies and body parts after death: the general common law rule

Dead bodies are legally odd things. They are not people, but neither are they simple property.

It is classically said that there is no property in a corpse. Grave robbers who made off with the corpse in a shroud could be charged with theft of the shroud but not of the body.

It is not quite as simple as that. If one does something to a body or a body part which changes its nature, the body or part is transformed into property. Thus if a body is preserved in formalin and its vessels injected with latex the body can be stolen. This is often cited as an exception to the general rule; it might not really be so. Although it might be possible now to put on the indictment that a body has been stolen, perhaps the allegation is really that formalin or latex has been stolen. It would be interesting to see if

---

18. [1991] Fam 33, at 46.
19. *Supra*, at 867.

an entirely unpreserved leg upon which the loving care of a dissector has been lavished would be property for these purposes.

## Use of parts of dead bodies for transplantation

The law is now contained in the Human Tissue Act 1961 (amended by the Corneal Tissue Act 1986).

Almost the whole story is contained in ss.1(1) and 1(2) of the 1961 Act, which provide:

*"(1)   If any person, either in writing at any time or orally in the presence of two or more witnesses during his last illness, has expressed a request that his body or any specified part of his body be used after his death for therapeutic purposes or for purposes of medical education or research, the person lawfully in possession of his body after his death may ... authorise the removal from the body of any part ... for use in accordance with the request.*

*(2)   Without prejudice to the foregoing subsection the person lawfully in possession of the body of a deceased person may authorise the removal of any part from the body for use for the said purposes if, having made such reasonable enquiry as may be practicable, he has no reason to believe:*

*(a)   that the deceased had expressed an objection to his body being so dealt with after his death, and had not withdrawn it; or*

*(b)   that the surviving spouse or any surviving relative of the deceased objects to the body being so dealt with."*

There remain several unanswered questions about these provisions. They include the questions: Who is lawfully in possession of the body before it is handed to the executors? Is there any sanction for breach?

The brain stem death criterion of death applies to the interpretation of the 1961 Act just as it does to other areas of law. The Department of Health has suggested that removing organs from a brain stem dead donor whose heart is still beating amounts to a battery. This is plainly wrong.

## Taking organs from live donors

Forgetting statute for a moment, the first issue is that of consent. A competent adult can consent to anything which does not amount to serious bodily injury. By this is meant serious bodily injury with no therapeutic benefit. Lots of organ donations will amount to serious bodily injury. It is surprising that it is not more strenuously argued in the legal literature that a kidney, for instance, cannot generally be donated lawfully. It is possible to imagine exceptions. For instance it may be lawful to give a kidney to save the life of a child related to the donor where there is evidence that the death or disease of the child would have a significant effect on the donor if the donor did not think that he had tried to help.

There are tissues which the common law of consent uncontroversially allows donation of. Obvious examples include blood and bone marrow. Blood also does not fall within the Human Organ Transplants Act, and the better view is that bone marrow does not either. If the common law of consent places such tight strictures even on the ability of competent adults to donate organs, still more tight are the restrictions on incompetent adults and minors.

As has been seen in the chapter on consent, the "best interests" test is applied in deciding on the legality of any medical intervention involving children or incompetent adults. In the case of children or incompetent adults this test applies to any medical intervention – not just those which would cause serious bodily injury. The donation of blood and bone marrow would, therefore, only be lawful if the donation passed this test. There will be few cases where donation can be said to be in the donor's best interests. Again there will be exceptions – for instance where a marrow donation would save the life of a sibling. The donor's life is likely to be affected much more profoundly by the death of the sibling than by the removal of the marrow.

Note that s.8 of the Family Law Reform Act 1969,[20] which provides that the consent to treatment of 16 and 17 year-olds should be treated like the consent of adults, applies only to therapeutic procedures. It cannot extend to the donation of organs (although it would be interesting to see if the courts regarded the therapeutic benefit of the survival of a sibling as sufficiently therapeutic to make consent to the donation of marrow valid under s.8).

On all this is superimposed the Human Organ Transplants Act 1989.

The Act defines "organ" as "any part of a human body consisting of a structured arrangement of tissues which, if wholly removed, cannot be replicated by the body."[21] This definition is clearly intended to exclude blood and, probably, bone marrow. It is possible to argue, with a straight face, that bone marrow does not qualify. There are two arguable reasons. The first is because, although it is anatomically disparate, it is histologically coherent, and is, therefore, "a structured arrangement of cells". And second, because if you take out all of it, you remove the stem cells which allow for its replacement, and incidentally kill the patient – a fairly definite way of ensuring no future replication. But probably a court

---

20. See Chapter 2.
21. Section 1(2).

would conclude that bone marrow was not a "structured arrangement of cells".

Section 1(1) of the Act speaks for itself. It says:

"*A person is guilty of an offence if in Great Britain he:*

*(a) makes or receives any payment for the supply of, or for an offer to supply, an organ which has been or is to be removed from a dead or living person and is intended to be transplanted into another person whether in Great Britain or elsewhere;*

*(b) seeks to find a person willing to supply for payment such an organ as is mentioned in para. (a) above or offers to supply such an organ for payment;*

*(c) initiates or negotiates any arrangement involving the making of any payment for the supply of, or for an offer to supply, such an organ; or*

*(d) takes part in the management or control of a body of persons corporate or unincorporate whose activities consist of or include the initiation or negotiation of such arrangements."*

The aim is clear. It seeks to ban commercial trafficking in organs. Section 1(2) extends the prohibition to advertising for organs for purposes prohibited by s.1(1). "Payment" means "payment in money or money's worth". It does not include a payment for defraying or reimbursing "the cost of removing, transporting or preserving the organ to be supplied" or "any expenses or loss of earnings incurred by a person so far as reasonably and directly attributable to his supplying an organ from his body".[22] No offence is therefore committed by placing an advertisement in a paper

---

22. Section 1(3).

asking for somebody to donate a kidney gratuitously and offering to pay his travel expenses and his loss of earnings.

Any removal of any organ is obviously dangerous. So is the insertion into a donee of any organ. Organ donation is much more likely to be successful if the donee is genetically related to the donor. The Act seeks to reduce the risk of pointless donation and implantation by placing restrictions on the transfer of organs between unrelated people. A person is regarded for these purposes as genetically related to *"(a) his natural parents and children; (b) his brothers and sister of the whole or half blood; (c) the brothers and sisters of the whole or half blood of either of his natural parents; and (d) the natural children of his brothers and sisters of the whole or half blood or of the brothers and sisters of the whole or half blood of either of his natural parents."*[23]

---

23. Section 2(2).

# APPENDIX 1

# PARTICULARS OF CLAIM IN A CLINICAL NEGLIGENCE CASE

<u>IN THE HIGH COURT OF JUSTICE</u>          <u>Claim No.1234567</u>

<u>QUEEN'S BENCH DIVISION</u>

**BETWEEN:**

JOHN SMITH

<u>Claimant</u>

–and–

DEATHSHIRE HOSPITAL NHS TRUST

<u>Defendant</u>

------------------------------------
**PARTICULARS OF CLAIM**
------------------------------------

1. The Defendant is and was at all material times a National Health Service Trust which, pursuant to the National Health Service Act 1977 and the National Health Service and Community Care Act 1990 and subsequent and subordinate legislation, owed and owes a duty to manage the Deathshire Hospital ("the hospital") and was and is vicariously liable for the acts or omissions, while in the course of their employment or engagement at the hospital, of all medical, surgical, nursing and ancillary staff at the hospital.

*Appendix 1*

2. On 2 January 2003:
   (a) the Claimant started to experience pain in his right iliac fossa; and
   (b) vomited repeatedly.

3. At about 09.30 on 3 January 2003 he was seen by his general medical practitioner who referred him urgently to the Accident and Emergency Department of the hospital.

4. The general practitioner's referral letter concluded: "I feel that this man may be suffering from appendicitis."

5. The Claimant arrived at the Accident and Emergency Department of the hospital at 10.14 on 3 January 2003.

6. He was seen by a House Officer, Dr. Green, at 10.40.

7. Dr. Green:
   (a) noted the history which is set out at paragraph 2 above; and
   (b) failed to conduct any examination at all; and
   (c) discharged the Claimant home with no medication; and
   (d) told the Claimant: "There is nothing wrong with you. You should not be wasting my time".

8. The Claimant's condition continued to deteriorate, and at 02.15 on 4 January 2003 he was readmitted to the hospital where a ruptured appendix was diagnosed.

9. The Claimant underwent immediate surgery.

10. The Defendant, by its servants or agents, was negligent.

## PARTICULARS OF NEGLIGENCE

(a) If Dr. Green failed to read the referral letter, failing to read it.
(b) If Dr. Green did read the referral letter, failing adequately to heed the suggestion that the Claimant might be suffering from appendicitis.
(c) Failing to conduct any or any adequate clinical examination. An adequate examination would have included manual palpation of the lower abdomen.
(d) Failing to arrange for any further investigations. These should have included a white cell count and an ESR.
(e) Failing adequately to heed the history, which was suggestive of appendicitis.
(f) Discharging the Claimant home.
(g) Failing to admit the Claimant to hospital.
(h) Reassuring the Claimant that there was nothing wrong with him.
(i) If contrary to the Claimant's primary submission, it was appropriate to discharge him home, failing to tell him that if the pain persisted for more than another 4 hours he should attend hospital again.
(j) Failing to diagnose appendicitis.

11. By reason of the matters aforesaid the Claimant, who was born on 12 October 1953, has sustained personal injury, loss and damage.

## PARTICULARS OF CAUSATION

(a) Reading the referral letter would or should have indicated that the general practitioner was concerned about appendicitis. This was a reasonable concern; appendicitis needed to be excluded.
(b) Adequate clinical examination, including manual palpation of the lower abdomen, would have revealed rebound pain in the right iliac fossa, which would have been strongly suggestive of appendicitis.
(c) The white cell count would have been raised, as would the ESR, suggesting infection.
(d) If appendicitis had been suspected as it should have been from the clinical findings, the investigations, the history and the referral letter,

*Appendix 1*

the Claimant would or should have been admitted to hospital where he would have undergone simple appendectomy by 12.30 on 3 January 2003. He would have avoided rupture of the appendix and would have been discharged home by 5 January. He would have been back to work by 15 January and would have had no long-term complications.

(e) If the Claimant had not been falsely reassured that there was nothing wrong with him and/or told that if the pain continued for more than 4 hours he should attend the Accident and Emergency Department again, he would have attended the hospital again by 15.00 on 3 January 2003. Appendicitis would have been diagnosed shortly thereafter, he would have undergone a simple appendectomy by 17.00 on 3 January 2003 and the clinical course and prognosis would have been as set out at paragraph 11(d) above.

## PARTICULARS OF PERSONAL INJURIES

(a) The appendix ruptured and by the time of the operation the Claimant had severe peritonitis. He underwent abdominal lavage.
(b) He was in the Intensive Care Unit until 6 January 2003, and was not discharged from hospital until 4 February 2003.
(c) He was unable to return to work until 4 June 2003.
(d) He has developed adhesions which cause him considerable pain. He is likely to need further surgery to break these adhesions down. The long-term prognosis is uncertain.
(e) Further details are set out in the report of Mr. Brown, Consultant Surgeon, dated 15 March 2004, a copy of which is annexed hereto.

## PARTICULARS OF SPECIAL DAMAGES

Particulars are set out in a separate schedule annexed hereto.

12. Further the Claimant is entitled to and claims interest on the sum found due to him for such period and at such rate as the court may think fit, pursuant to section 35A of the Supreme Court Act 1981.

AND the Claimant claims:

1. Damages.
2. Interest pursuant to statute as aforesaid.

**A. BARRISTER**

**SERVED this**            **day of**            **2004**

**By A. Solicitor, 23 High Street, Greater Carnage, Oxfordshire, OX14 5BY, Solicitors for the Claimant**

**STATEMENT OF TRUTH**

**I, John Smith, believe that the facts stated in these Particulars of Claim are true.**

**Signed** ................................

# APPENDIX 2

# DEFENCE IN A CLINICAL NEGLIGENCE CASE

<u>IN THE HIGH COURT OF JUSTICE</u>　　　<u>Claim No. 1234567</u>

<u>QUEEN'S BENCH DIVISION</u>

**BETWEEN:**

**JOHN SMITH**

<u>Claimant</u>

–and–

**DEATHSHIRE HOSPITAL NHS TRUST**

<u>Defendant</u>

---------------
**DEFENCE**
---------------

1. In this Defence, whenever anything is said to be not admitted, the Defendant does not know whether it is true or not, and requires the Claimant to prove it.[1]

2. As to paragraph 2 of the Particulars of Claim:
   (a) No admissions are made as to the truth of these allegations.

---

1. A sop to the Civil Procedure Rules, which, on one reading, require a very convoluted form of words instead of the simple "not admitted" or "no admissions".

(b) The pleaded allegations are consistent with the history given in the referral letter and to the history given to Dr. Green at the consultation on 3 January 2003.

3. As to paragraph 3 of the Particulars of Claim:
   (a) No admissions are made as to the time when the Claimant was seen by his general medical practitioner.
   (b) Save as aforesaid this paragraph is admitted.

4. Paragraphs 4, 5 and 6 of the Particulars of Claim are admitted.

5. As to paragraph 7 of the Particulars of Claim:
   (a) Paragraph 7(a) is admitted.
   (b) As to paragraph. 7(b):
      (i) This is denied.
      (ii) A full clinical examination was performed, which included manual palpation of the lower abdomen.
      (iii) No abnormalities were found.
      (iv) In particular there was no rebound tenderness in the right iliac fossa.
   (c) As to paragraph 7(c):
      (i) This is admitted.
      (ii) There was no indication for admission, and no indication for any medication.
   (d) Paragraph 7(d) is denied.

8. As to paragraph 8 of the Particulars of Claim:
   (a) No admissions are made as to the Claimant's condition between discharge on 3 January and re-admission on 4 January.
   (b) Save as aforesaid this paragraph is admitted.

9. Paragraph 9 of the Particulars of Claim is admitted.

10. As to paragraph 10 of the Particulars of Claim, it is denied that the Defendant, by its servants or agents, was negligent as alleged or at all.

*Appendix 2*

11. Without prejudice to the generality of the foregoing denial, the Defendant pleads to the allegations of negligence as follows:
    (a) *As to Particulars of Negligence (a) and (b):*
        (i) Dr. Green did read the letter.
        (ii) He noted and took appropriate heed of the suggestion that the Claimant might be suffering from appendicitis.
        (iii) He conducted his own clinical assessment and appropriately (although, as it turned out, wrongly) concluded that the Claimant was not suffering from appendicitis.
    (b) *As to Particulars of Negligence (c)*
        Paragraphs 5(b)(ii) and 5(b)(iii) of this Defence are repeated.
    (c) *As to Particulars of Negligence (d)*
        Given the clinical findings, no further investigations were indicated.
    (d) *As to Particulars of Negligence (e), (f) and (g)*
        (i) The history was heeded adequately.
        (ii) It is accepted that the history was consistent with appendicitis.
        (iii) It is denied that the history was suggestive of appendicitis.
        (iv) The history with which the Claimant presented is a very common one. In the huge majority of cases with such a history there is no appendicitis.
        (v) Dr. Green was entitled, given his findings on clinical examination, to conclude that no further examination, investigation or treatment was indicated, and that admission was unnecessary.
    (e) *As to Particulars of Negligence (h)*
        (i) It is admitted that this reassurance was given.
        (ii) Given the clinical findings it was appropriate to give it.
    (f) *As to Particulars of Negligence (i)*
        (i) It is admitted that no such suggestion was made.
        (ii) There was no indication for such a suggestion. Given the clinical findings, any continued pain was likely to subside over the next 24 hours and was not likely to indicate any condition which demanded hospital treatment.

(g) *As to Particulars of Negligence (j)*
   (i) It is admitted that no diagnosis of appendicitis was made.
   (ii) For the reasons set out in paragraphs 11(a) and 11(d) of this Defence it was reasonable not to diagnose appendicitis.
(h) *Generally*
   At all material times Dr. Green acted in accordance with a responsible body of medical opinion in Accident and Emergency Medicine.

12. As to the Particulars of Causation in paragraph 11 of the Particulars of Claim:
   (a) *As to Particulars of Causation (a)*
      Paragraph 11(a) of this Defence is repeated.
   (b) *As to Particulars of Causation (b)*
      Paragraph 5(b) of this Defence is repeated.
   (c) *As to Particulars of Causation (c)*
      (i) It is not admitted that either the white cell count and the ESR would have been raised.
      (ii) If either had been raised, the elevation would not have been sufficient to demand further investigation.
   (d) *As to Particulars of Causation (d)*
      (i) If the Claimant had been admitted immediately and appendicitis diagnosed then or shortly afterwards, he would have been observed on the general surgical ward.
      (ii) The operating list on 3 January 2003 was very busy. It would have been impossible for the Claimant to have undergone surgery at the hospital before he in fact did.
      (iii) The Claimant's condition would not have been sufficiently serious to warrant transferring him to another hospital for surgery.
   (e) *As to Particulars of Causation (e)*
      (i) No admissions are made as to what the Claimant would or would not have done.
      (ii) Paragraph 12(d) of this Defence is repeated, and accordingly this allegation is causally irrelevant.

*Appendix 2*

13. As to the Particulars of Personal Injuries in paragraph 11 of the Particulars of Claim:
    (a) Paragraphs 13(a) and 13(b) are admitted.
    (b) Save as aforesaid no admissions are made.

14. As to the Particulars of Special Damages, a counter-schedule is served herewith.

15. As to paragraph 12 of the Particulars of Claim, no admissions are made to the Claimant's entitlement to interest on any sum found due to him.

**B. BARRISTER**

**SERVED this          day of          2004**

**By B. Solicitor, 123 Low Street, Even Greater Carnage, Oxfordshire, OX16 4GZ, Solicitors for the Defendant**

**STATEMENT OF TRUTH**

**I, John Brown, believe that the facts stated in this Defence are true.**

**Signed** ..............................

# INDEX

abortion 10, 15-19
  compulsory disclosure 77
  ECHR 27, 29, 30, 31
  fetal rights 14-15
  intrauterine damage 19-22
  late 17-19
  wrongful birth 25
accidents 105-6
actual bodily harm 37, 38
AIDS 72-3
alternative medicine 108, 111-15
anaesthetists 18, 152
artificial nutrition and hydration (ANH) 59, 111, 158
  Bland, Tony 157, 158-62
  Burke, Leslie 169-70
assault 37-9, 41, 63, 165
  Bland, Tony 162
assisted reproduction 8-9, 32
  cloning 13-14
  designer embryos 11-12
  intrauterine damage 23-4
autonomy 5, 35, 39, 67, 171
  abortion 15
  conjoined twins 147

Baker, Sir George 14
battery 40-2, 174
best interests 55-7, 159, 166, 169-72

access to health records 81-2
Bland, Tony 159-63
conjoined twins 146-7, 149, 150
consent 36, 51-2, 54-8
live birth after late abortion 19
live transplant donors 174-5
resources 110-11
switching off 165
Bingham, Lord 155
birth 14, 28-32
  compulsory disclosure 77-8
  late abortion 18-19
  intrauterine damage 20-1
  wrongful 24-7
Bland, Tony 18, 36, 59, 107, 111, 156-65, 172
Blood, Diane 6
blood donation 174-5
bodies and body parts 7, 172-3
  transplants 173-7
*Bolam* test 100-8
  alternative medicine 112
  Bland, Tony 159-60
  breach of confidence 76
  causation 121-2
  consent 43-4, 46, 55-6, 65, 66, 109
  human rights 115-17, 166-7
  manslaughter 152

negligence 100-8, 109, 112, 115-17, 121-2, 141, 152
bone marrow donation 174-6
brain-damaged babies 19, 90, 91, 138, 139-40
brain death 142
brain stem death 142, 174
Bland, Tony 158, 160
Brandon, Lord 55
Bristow J 41-2, 59
British Medical Association (BMA) guidelines 107
British Standards Institution 105-6
Brooke LJ 119-20, 145-9, 151-2
Brown LJ, Simon 2, 74, 121
Browne-Wilkinson, Lord 44, 101-3, 109
burden and standard of proof 117-20
   loss of a chance 128-9
Burke, Leslie 61-3, 65, 169-70
Butler-Sloss LJ 56, 161, 166-9

cancer 124-6
causation 42, 120-34
   defence 186
   limitation 136
   loss of a chance 122-31
   multiple causes 131-4
   negligence 42, 120-34, 180-1, 186
   particulars of claim 180-1
cerebral palsy 19, 90, 140
Chief Medical Officer 77, 138

Child Support 8
children 51-4
   abortion 16
   assisted reproduction 8-9
   consent 36, 51-4
   designer embryos 10-12
   genetics 5, 6-8
   live transplant donors 174-5
   negligence 97, 138, 139-40
   sperm conversion 6-8
civil law 32, 40-8, 79-81, 85
   abortion 18
   consent 36, 40-8
   intrauterine damage 20
   ownership of gametes 7-8
clinical audit 47
cloning 1, 6, 13-14, 32
common law
   abortion 14
   access to health records 81-2
   Bland, Tony 158
   confidentiality 2, 67, 81-2, 84, 86
   consent 35, 46
   death 142, 172-3
   intrauterine damage 19-21
   live transplant donors 174
   manslaughter 154
   necessity 151
   negligence 99
   right to reject or demand treatment 171
   use of bodies after death 172-3
compensation
   intrauterine damage 19, 22

# Index

loss of a change 122-4, 126-8, 130
negligence 41, 43, 95, 139-40, 153
psychiatric injury 95
trespass to the person 41-2
wrongful birth 25, 26
*see also* damages
competence (capacity) 49-57, 165, 170-2
consent 35-6, 47, 49-57, 59, 63-4
live transplant donors 174-5
compulsory disclosure 77-82
compulsory treatment 61, 66
conditional fees 89
confidentiality 1, 2-4, 67-87
breach 67, 68-77
statutes 77-87
conjoined twins 20, 145-52, 162
conscience 2-3, 68, 74-6, 92
consciousness 142, 166-9
Bland, Tony 161
consent 57-8, 64
switching off 165
consent 35-66, 109
abortion 17
best interests 36, 51-2, 54-8
breach of confidence 68-70
children 36, 51-4
civil proceedings 36, 40-8
competence or capacity 35-6, 47, 49-57, 59, 63-4
compulsory disclosure 79, 82
conjoined twins 145

criminal proceedings 36-40
disciplinary jurisdiction 48-9
euthanasia 144
forms 58-9
human rights 35, 60-6
implied 57-8, 69
informed 39, 42-8, 65-6
live transplant donors 174-5
mental health 35, 50, 54-7
necessity 57-8
negligence 40, 41, 42-8, 49, 63, 108, 109, 117
trespass to the person 40-2, 53, 59
consumer law 135
contempt of court 72
contraception 52
contract law 99-100
hospitals 96
loss of a chance 122-3, 126
product liability 134
costs in negligence cases 89-90
Court of Cassation 29
crime prevention 70-2, 74, 86
criminal law 36-40, 148-51
abortion 15, 18
conjoined twins 146, 148-51
consent 36-40
manslaughter 155
ownership of gametes 7-8
Crown Indemnity 91

damages
aggravated 41-2
breach of confidence 68
causation 120

191

criminal sanctions 30
defence 187
intrauterine damage 19, 24
live birth after late abortion 18
loss of a chance 122-3, 125-6, 130
negligence 41-3, 90-1, 95, 98-9, 116, 120, 122, 181-2, 187
particulars of claim 181-2
psychiatric injury 95
sperm conversion 8
trespass to the person 41-2
unlawful invasion 159
wrongful birth 26
*see also* compensation
deafness 22-3, 24
death 142-77
  access to health records 82
  Bland, Tony 156-65
  body parts 7, 172-4
  conjoined twins 145-52
  human rights 166-9
  keeping patients alive 169-72
  manslaughter 152-6
  murder and euthanasia 143-4
  switching off 156-65
  transplantation 173-7
defence of others 148, 150
dentists and dentistry 37-8, 42, 53, 97
Department of Health guidelines 107
diagnosis 12-13, 44, 101, 109
  loss of a chance 124-7

Dica, Mohammed 38
disability 40-1, 55-6, 66
  abortion 16-17
  intrauterine damage 20-4
  limitation 138
  suing for existence 20
  wrongful birth 25-6
disciplinary codes 2, 36, 48-9
DNA 1
doctor-patient relationship 92, 93, 96-7
Donaldson MR, Lord 53, 172
double effect 143, 152
  conjoined twins 148, 150
  trolley problem 165
drug abuse and compulsory treatment 61

Egdell, Dr 70-2, 74
embryos 9-13, 14-34
  cloning 13-14
  designer 10-12
  ECHR 27-34
  intrauterine damage 19-24
  pre-implantation diagnosis 21-13
  surplus 9, 11, 14
  *see also* fetuses
emergency care 96-7
Erle CJ 119
ethics 5, 32-3
  alternative medicine 112
  Bland, Tony 163, 165
  confidentiality 4, 75-6
  conjoined twins 149
  consent 44-5, 49

# Index

intrauterine damage 24
murder and euthanasia 143
resources 109, 111
European Group on Ethics in Science and New Technologies 32
euthanasia 143-4, 151, 163, 170, 171-2
evidence 89, 117-20, 121, 132, 156
   alternative medicine 112, 114
   *Bolam* test 100-5
evidence-based medicine 104-8, 115
expert witnesses 89, 121, 156
   alternative medicine 112, 114
   *Bolam* test 101-5

family law 8, 59, 146-8
   conjoined twins 146-9, 150, 151
fetuses 14-34
   24 week 10, 16-17
   abortion 14-19
   ECHR 27-34
   intrauterine damage 19-24
   *see also* embryos
financial gain 37
force feeding 63-4

gametes 6-8, 23
General Medical Council 48-9, 101, 170
   confidentiality 3, 71, 74, 76

consent 39, 44-5, 47, 48-9
general practitioners 92, 108
   alternative medicine 112-13
   negligence 91, 92, 112-13
Genetic Commissioning Advisory Group 13
genetics 1-6
   cloning 13
   compulsory disclosure 78
   defects 12
   designer embryos 10-12
   differentiation 10
   disability 22-3
   ECHR 32
   ownership of gametes 6-8
   pre-implantation diagnosis 12-13
   transplantation 177
Gillick, Victoria 52
*Gillick* competency 51, 52-3, 54
Goff, Lord 36, 57, 107, 172
Grand Chamber 31
grievous bodily harm 37, 38, 143
gross negligence manslaughter 18, 152-6
guidelines and protocols 104-8, 170

Hale LJ 127-8, 130-1
Hashmi, Zain 10-13
health records disclosure 81-2, 85
hepatitis 135-6
Hewart CJ, Lord 153

Hillsborough disaster 95, 157
HIV 38
Hobhouse LJ 117-19
Hoffmann, Lord 125, 127, 129
Hope LJ 125
hospitals 97, 134, 139, 145, 170
House of Lords 107
   Bland, Tony 157-8
   cloning 13
   consent 43, 52, 59, 66
   fetal rights 15
   *Gillick* competency 52
   loss of a chance 123-5, 127
   manslaughter 154
   multiple causes 132-4
   negligence 43, 120-2, 123-5
   shipwreck case 149, 151-2
   wrongful birth 26
Human Fertilisation and Embryology Authority (HFEA) 9, 11-13
   cloning 13-14
   disability 23
   licences 12-13
Human Genetics Commission 1
human rights 60-6, 115-17, 166-9
   consent 35, 60-6
   ECHR 27-34

Iceland 4
injunctions 72-3, 77
insurance 89, 90, 91, 129
intellectual property 1, 5-6
intention
   murder 143-4, 148, 150, 152
   trolley problem 165
   withdrawal of treatment 166

Jehovah's Witnesses 40
Joffe, Lord 144
Johnson J 145
judicial review 11, 98, 170

Latham LJ 127
Law Commission 21
legal aid 88
legal personality 30-1
Legal Services Commission 88
life expectancy 131
limitation 136-8
loss of a chance 122-31

Malette, Mrs 40
manslaughter 18, 152-6, 165
   unintentional 29-30
margin of appreciation 116
   ECHR 29, 32-4
maternal and fetal rights conflict 27-8, 30-1
McNair J 100
Medical Defence Union 91
Medical and Dental Defence Union of Scotland 91
Medical Ethics Committee 107
Medical Protection Society 91
*mens rea* 150-1, 155, 162
mental health 54-7, 171
   abortion 16, 17
   breach of confidence 70-2
   compulsory disclosure 79, 82

## Index

consent 35, 50, 54-7
euthanasia 144
hospitals 97
switching off 165
motive 143, 165
Munby J 169-72
murder 143-4
   Bland, Tony 157-8, 162-3
   conjoined twins 145, 148, 150-2, 162
   shipwreck 148-9, 151
   trolley problem 164-5
   withdrawal of treatment 162

National Health Service 3, 96-9, 169-70
   health records 81, 85
   human rights 168
   negligence 89-91, 96-9, 116, 123, 139-41, 178
National Health Service Litigation Authority (NHSLA) 89-90, 139
National Health Service Redress Scheme 139-41
national security 80, 86
necessity 57-8, 62-3, 148-9, 151
needle phobia 35, 51
negligence 42-8, 88-141, 178-82
   alternative medicine 111-15
   burden or standard of proof 117-20
   causation 42, 120-34, 180-1, 186

claimants 88-9
consent 40, 41, 42-8, 49, 63, 108, 109, 117
costs 89-90
defence 183-7
defendants 89-91
duty owed 92-100
euthanasia 144
future 138-41
human rights 115-17
intrauterine damage 19-20
limitation 136-8
loss of a chance 122-31
manslaughter 18, 152-6
multiple causes 131-4
omissions 96, 133, 136, 144, 152
product liability 134-6
proving breach of duty 100-15
wrongful birth 25
Newey QC, HHJ 106
Nicholls LJ 125, 127-8
no-fault liability 138-9
notifiable diseases 77
nurses' station 69

pain 143-4, 157
   conjoined twins 146-7, 148, 151
palliative care 144
parental responsibility 51, 54, 62
particulars of claim 99, 178-82
   defence 183-7
patents 5-6

Patients' Charter 81
persistent vegetative state (PVS)
    59, 107, 111, 143, 166-9
    Bland, Tony 157-8, 160-2
personal injury 88, 181
    defence 187
    intrauterine damage 20
    limitation 136-7
    loss of a chance 125, 130
    particulars of claim 180,
        181
personal records 79, 83
pharmacists 2, 74-5
Phillips LJ 125, 129-30
phobias 35, 50-1
plastic surgery 99-100
police 78-9
Primary Care Trust 92
private medical care 91, 99,
    103, 139, 141
    loss of a chance 123
product liability 134-6
Professional Conduct
    Committee 49
property law 1, 7-8, 15, 70,
    172-3
psychiatric injury 94-5
public domain 68, 76-7
public interest 70, 74
    confidentiality 3, 68, 70-4,
        76
    disclosure 79-81, 84
    immunity 79-81
public law 110
public policy 21, 25, 39, 123
public safety 61

Quintavelle, Josephine 11-12

reasonable patient test 44-5, 46,
    48, 66
recklessness 39, 155
refusal of treatment 51-2
    consent 35-6, 41, 49-50,
        51-2, 53-4
Register of Chinese Herbal
    Medicine 112
Reid, Lord 155
resources 109-11, 168
    negligence 108, 109-11, 116
right to life 28, 30, 32-3,
    115-16, 166-7
    Bland, Tony 160
    conjoined twins 146-7
road traffic 4, 61, 78, 155
Rodger, Lord 132-3
Rose J 72-4
Royal College of Paediatrics and
    Child Health 106

Scarman, Lord 35, 52, 102
self-defence 148, 150
Senate of Surgery 44-5
sensitive personal data 83
serious professional misconduct
    49
sexual molestation 36, 38
sexually transmitted diseases 4,
    37-9
shipwreck case 148-9, 151
sperm 6-8, 23
standard of care 100-4
    alternative medicine 112-14

## Index

guidelines 104-8
   negligence 100-8, 112-14
state of the art defence 135-6
stem cells 9-11, 13-14, 175
Stephenson LJ 21-2
sterilisation 25, 55, 59
Stuart-Smith LJ 105
succession rights 15
switching off 156-65

Templeman LJ 35, 73, 80
terrorism 78
Thorpe LJ 56-7
torts
   breach of confidence 67, 68-77
   causation 120, 122-3, 125-7, 129
   contractual duties 99-100
   hospitals 96-7
   intrauterine damage 24
   loss of a chance 122-3, 125-7, 129
   negligence 41, 92, 94-7, 99-100, 120, 122, 139
   primary and secondary victims 95-6
   trespass to the person 40
traditional Chinese herbal medicine (TCHM) 112

transplants 173-4, 176
   live donors 174-7
trespass to the person 40-2
   consent 40-2, 53, 59
trolley problem 159, 163-5

unintentional homicide 29-30

vaccination 61, 65, 105
Vo, Mrs 29-30, 32
Voluntary Euthanasia Society 171-2

Walker LJ, Robert 145, 147, 150, 151-2
Ward LJ 145-52
wards of court 52, 54
warning of risks 42-8, 60
   *Bolam* test 101, 109
withdrawal of treatment 117, 165, 166
   Bland, Tony 157, 158-62
   conjoined twins 147
witness summons 79, 80
Woolf, Lord 48, 88, 138, 140
Working Party on the Protection of the Human Embryo and Fetus 32
wrongful birth 24-7
wrongful life 20-4